Prais
LIGHTEN YOUR **LOAD**

"Lighten Your Load: 35 Surprisingly Simple Ways to Free Your-self from Stress, Toxins, and Clutter, is a pleasurable and enjoyable little book that helps you put what's important first and everything else last."

– Will Bowen, #1 International Bestselling Author
and Founder of A Complaint Free World

"Sometimes the things that can impact you most are also the simplest. Follow the instructions in this book, and I guarantee that your life will be transformed. There's more straightforward good advice – and wise practice – in these pages than in any self-help book I've ever seen."

– Caitriona Reed, author, speaker
and co-founder of Five Changes

"Lighten Your Load is a great read for anyone looking to get started on the path of detoxing their life and body. Karin Kiser is humorous, encouraging, and honest as she offers applicable changes we can make in many areas of our lives."

– Lane B. Freeman, DDS, Biological dentist at Nunnally and Freeman, Marble Falls, Texas

"Karin Kiser's enthusiastic suggestions for 'lightening your load' really inspire and enlighten the reader. I look forward to recommending her book to all of my clients."

– Kim Krost, owner of Integrative Healing Institute

LIGHTEN YOUR
LOAD

35 Surprisingly Simple Ways to Free Yourself From Stress, Toxins, and Clutter

KARIN KISER

**Camino
Chronicles
PRESS**

Camino Chronicles Press
9450 Mira Mesa Blvd, Suite 320
San Diego, CA 92126

This book has been registered with the Library of Congress.

Printed in the United States of America

*To my sister Kim, and to all
those with the courage to
lighten their loads.*

Note to Readers

This publication contains the opinions and ideas of its author. It is intended to provide helpful and informative material on the subjects addressed. The strategies outlined in this book may not be suitable for every individual and are not guaranteed or warranted to produce any particular results.

This book is sold with the understanding that neither the author nor the publisher is engaged in rendering medical or other professional advice or services. The reader should consult a competent professional before adopting any of the suggestions in this book or drawing inferences from it.

No warranty is made with respect to the accuracy or completeness of the information or references contained herein, and both the author and the publisher specifically disclaim any responsibility for any liability, loss or risk, personal or otherwise, which is incurred as a consequence, directly or indirectly, by the use and application of any of the contents of this book.

Contents

Stop!

Before You Start Reading, Get Your FREE Gifts...

- The Top 5 Tips To Implement Now
- The Lighten Your Load Success Tracker
- Your Special 5 Minute Guided Meditation

Each of These 3 Free Gifts Will Help You On Your Journey To Lighten Your Load.

To Get Them Visit:
http://karinkiser.com/free-gifts/

INTRODUCTION

You're always on the go – but lately you're feeling drained, tired, or stressed out.

You're super busy – but truth be told, you're not actually enjoying your jam-packed days.

You're a high achiever – but find it challenging to balance work life and home life.

You're smart – but that's part of the problem. At the end of your day, you can't shut off your mind, so it's nearly impossible to relax and recharge.

If this sounds like you, you're in good company. This is actually one of the biggest problems we face in modern life:

- We love our full days but tend to over-schedule ourselves.

- We love being on the go but don't give ourselves time to be still.

- We love our gadgets until somehow their beeps, pings, and dings end up running our lives!

The trouble is, living this way takes its toll – on your health, your waistline, your energy, your joy, and your ability to stay calm and think clearly, especially when things get messy.

The good news is, you *can* have more energy, less stress, more time, and greater ease when you *Lighten Your Load.*

I know this because I've done it. I know all about stress. I used to work 70+ hours a week. I used to think the formula for success and happiness was to "just work harder and get more done."

Not anymore. I lightened my load. You can too.

Don't worry. I'm not going to suggest you lighten your load by working only part time, delegating all your responsibilities, downsizing to a small apartment, or moving to an ashram. If this were desirable or possible for you, you would likely be doing it already.

Lightening your load simply means reducing the toxin buildup that has – over the years and perhaps even decades – crept into your body, your home, and your thoughts.

What is this toxin buildup?

It's the clutter, negativity, and other gunk that slowly creep into our lives. Think about the stuff that collects in your bathtub drain or the grime that ends up on your sunglasses. Or the dust bunny colonies that seem to appear out of nowhere. You know what I'm talking about. Well, your body accumulates nasty buildup as well. So does your mind.

Left unattended, these toxins build up. They take up space. They get stuck in your body, your mind, and your personal environment.

Fortunately, there are countless ways to *Lighten Your Load.* This book offers 35 of them – 35 simple yet profound ways to reduce the stress, toxins, and clutter that are literally weighing you down.

When you *Lighten Your Load* of toxin buildup, you feel more energetic, more at ease, and more alive.

You sleep better.

You think more clearly.

You begin to notice a greater sense of calm, regardless of what is going on around you.

It's hard to live the life you were meant to – one of balance, peace, ease, and joy – if your body and mind are overloaded with stress, toxins, and clutter. There's no need to spend another day feeling overwhelmed, rushed, or worn out. It's time to *Lighten Your Load.*

In fact, it's critical. You'll see why in the next chapter.

1 | THE ROOT CAUSE OF STRESS

Stress. We all have it. You could probably easily list 10 things that are adding stress to your day.

We are surrounded by books, blogs, and pills to help us manage our stress. There is something wrong with that. Manage stress. Why would we want to simply *manage* stress when we can reduce it? The whole idea of managing stress assumes that stress is a mandatory part of life – that it's here to stay – so the best we can do is learn to manage it.

Baloney!

Sure, there are things you can do to manage stress, just like there are pills you can take to manage physical pain. But why manage it when you can get to the root of why it is happening in the first place? The root cause of stress is not other people. It's not your job, your finances, or anything outside of you. These are just symptoms. Stress is a symptom of something deeper.

That deeper, root cause of stress is often the toxin buildup that creeps its way into our bodies, minds, and personal space. For most of us, this process starts early. I know this from personal experience.

As a child, I grew up eating processed food and junk: ice cream, chips, and all things canned, boxed, frozen, or fried. Because I was thin and active, I believed I could eat whatever I wanted as long as I worked out. I rarely thought about the quality of the food. Little did I know, my body was accumulating physical toxins.

As an adolescent, along with poor eating habits, I picked up a number of limiting beliefs about myself and the world around me. I believed that struggle and hard work were a normal part of life, and if you wanted to achieve anything, you had to figure it out on your own. This "me" focus and the need to do it all myself had its downside, namely anger, negativity, and stress.

It turns out there's more to toxins and clutter than a crowded closet or a constipated colon. What we put in, on, and around our bodies and minds can also add to the load.

There are actually five main areas where stress, toxins, and clutter tend to build up in our lives.

1. *Cellular gunk*: We all know that what we eat and drink eventually exits the body as waste. But did you know that the individual cells of your body produce waste too? Just like the waste in your colon, the waste from your cells also needs a way out!

2. *Physical toxins:* Most of us have hundreds of foreign compounds in our body. How do we get them? We eat them, drink them, breathe them, and slather them on our skin. Who knew? The gunk we actively put in and on our body makes up the physical toxins and stressors.

3. *Environmental clutter:* Got an overflowing car trunk or a Negative Nelly for a coworker? How about 14 electrical gadgets in your bedroom or a dozen chemical cleaners in your kitchen? These are examples of toxic buildup in your personal environment.

4. *Mental clutter:* Negativity, pessimism, and complaining are mental toxins. So are most forms of media. What types of blogs, television, and radio programs do you regularly consume? How much of it uplifts you, teaches you something useful, or contributes to your overall joy? All the rest is mental clutter.

5. *Emotional toxins:* Got anger, fear, or sadness? Are you holding a grudge or do you have an unresolved issue with a family member? Yep, these are emotional toxins.

These five types of toxins and clutter are essentially "life garbage" that you accumulate over time. It weighs you down. It stresses you out. It can also wreak havoc in your life.

In my case, my body had been trying to tell me for years that my toxic load was too high. I received the call to "wake up" many times and in many ways. Like most people, I didn't recognize the calls at first. I believed a serious car accident in my teens was "just bad luck," passing out many times over the years was "just dehydration," getting melanoma in my 20s was "a genetic predisposition." It took a serious fall that nearly killed me to delve deeper into what was really going on.

After years of trial and error, I learned that I was poisoning myself with this toxic "life garbage" – a.k.a. stress, negativity, poor eating habits, and anger.

It was time to take another approach to life. My transformation had begun.

I changed my diet and began to question everything I put in and on my body. I questioned the type of media I exposed myself to, the people I surrounded myself with, my thoughts, my beliefs, everything. I went to wellness conferences and read countless books. I studied nutrition, herbs, bodywork, energy work, longevity, and the mind-body connection. What I discovered was this…

Mental and emotional toxins are equally, if not more, destructive than the physical toxins we eat and drink.
Taking out this garbage is key to lightening your load so you can have more energy, mental clarity, and ease.

Why wait for a mental, physical, financial, or relationship crisis to modify bad habits when you can upgrade those things and *Lighten Your Load* now?

You don't have to experience physical trauma or unexplained health issues like I did to realize you have toxic habits and behaviors. In the next chapter, you'll see how heavy your load *really* is with a handy self-test.

Then in Chapters Three through Seven, we will dive into the 35 ways to free your life of stress, toxins, and clutter. I have personally used each of these strategies. Although there are countless others, these 35 made the cut because they are easy to implement and offer profound results. Just incorporating a handful of them consistently over time can transform your life.

Finally, in Chapter Eight, we will bring it all together and celebrate the lighter, happier, healthier YOU.

For best results, I invite you to read through the entire book first, since the strategies in each chapter build on each other. Then go back and put into action whichever strategies resonate most with you.

Warning: You might think some of these 35 ways are simple. You might have heard of them before. Don't be fooled by simple. Knowing *about* something and actually doing it on a daily basis is not so simple. The simple stuff is often, dare I say, radical.

You might also think some of the strategies are impractical, especially the ones involving technology. The mind will look for objections. You may find yourself thinking, "Yes, well, that will never work with my family," or "Easy for you to say, you don't have five children, an ailing parent, or my work schedule." Rather than looking for reasons it *won't* work for your particular situation, consider instead how it *could* work. How could you experiment with that strategy for one week? What might be possible then?

One final thing before we dig in. This book is intentionally short. The last thing you want to do when you're stressed out is add a 400-page book to your life.

Let's get started.

2 | THE SELF-TEST – HOW HEAVY IS YOUR LOAD?

Just how heavy is your load of stress, toxins, and clutter? Take this 20-question quiz to find out. Select the response most appropriate to your situation and then note the number of points in the space to the right.

1. Do you have a to-do list with more than 10 things on it?
   - Yes (+5 points)
   - No (-3 points)

   My points _____

2. How often do you use your microwave?
   - More than once per day (+5 points)
   - Once a day (+4 points)
   - 1-2 times per week (+2 points)
   - Never (-5 points)

   My points _____

3. How many bowel movements do you have per day?
   - More than two (-5 points)
   - Two (-3 points)
   - One (+2 points)
   - Sometimes none (+5 points)

   My points _____

4. What color is your urine typically?
- Regular yellow (+2)
- Light yellow (-2)
- Dark yellow (+4)
- Darker than yellow (+5)

My points _____

5. Do you drink unfiltered tap water?
- Yes (+4)
- Sometimes (+2)
- Never (-4)

My points _____

6. What type of water do you shower or bathe in?
- Tap water through a shower head filter (-5)
- Tap water straight up (+5)
- Filtered water via whole-house system such as reverse osmosis (-5)

My points _____

7. How often do you catch a cold or get sick?
- Once a year (+2)
- Twice a year (+4)
- More than twice a year (+5)
- Once every few years (-2)
- Never (-5)

My points _____

8. On a scale of 1 to 10, what is your energy level on an average day?
- 1-3 = Low (+4)
- 4-5 = So-so (+3)
- 6-7 = Moderate (-1)
- 8-9 = Really good (-2)
- 10 = Excellent (-3)

My points _____

9. Do you meditate?
- Yes, every day (-5)
- Yes, a few times per week (-3)
- Occasionally (0)
- No (+4)

My points _____

10. When you are in the company of others, what percentage of that time is with positive, uplifting people?
- Less than 40% (+4)
- 40-70% (+2)
- More than 70% (-3)

My points _____

11. On average, how many hours per day do you spend in front of a computer, tablet, or smart phone?
- Less than 2 hours (-4)
- 2-4 hours (+2)
- More than 4 hours (+5)

My points _____

12. How many hours per day do you spend watching TV or surfing the net?
- Less than 2 (-2)
- 2-4 hours (+4)
- More than 4 hours (+5)

My points _____

13. Do you typically hold or are you currently holding a grudge against someone?
- Yes (+3)
- No (-3)

My points _____

14. How many things on your kitchen counter don't belong in the kitchen (for example, car keys, kids' homework, mail, random papers, or toys)?
- 5 or more (+5)
- 3-4 (+3)
- 1-2 (+1)
- None (-3)

My points _____

15. How many things are plugged into the walls of your bedroom?
- 5 or more (+4)
- 3-4 (+2)
- 1-2 (-2)
- None (-4)

My points _____

16. How often do you engage in activity that really makes you sweat?
- 3 or more times per week (-5)
- 2 times per week (-3)
- Once per week (0)
- Once or twice per month (+3)
- Less than once per month (+5)

My points _____

17. Do you have clothes in your closet that don't currently fit you (they're either too big or too small)?
- Yes (+3)
- No (-3)

My points _____

18. Do you have any of your belongings in storage (for example, in your parents' attic or in a rented storage unit?)
- Yes (+4)
- No (0)

My points _____

19. Do you turn your computer and your phone off at night?
    - Yes (-2)
    - No (+5)

                              My points _____

20. Do you have trouble sleeping?
    - Yes (+5)
    - Sometimes (+3)
    - No (-3)

                              My points _____

Add up your total points here

                              Total points _____

Your current load is….

Extra heavy (51 to 90 points): More points are definitely not better in this quiz. Bigger points mean a heavier load, and in your case, it's extra heavy. Don't worry, though, since worrying will just add to your points! This high score simply means you will have a lot of choices for lightening your load. Read on.

Heavy (11 to 50 points): Your load is not bursting at the seams just yet, but it's still pretty darn heavy. You've come to the right place!

Medium (-29 to 10): Not bad! In this day and age, having just a medium-sized load is actually quite an accomplishment. With just a few upgrades and new habits, you can quickly be on your way to a lighter, brighter you.

Light (-69 to -30): Negative scores are a good thing here. Well done! The good news is that no matter how light your load currently is, it can always get lighter. In the chapters ahead, you'll get some tips to reduce your load even further.

3 | LIGHTEN YOUR CELLULAR LOAD

Don't panic. Your cellular load has nothing to do with your smart phone. Here, cellular refers to the more than 30 trillion cells in your body.

We all know that what we eat and drink eventually exits the body as waste. But you may not realize that the cells of your body produce waste too. Just like the gunk in your colon, the waste from your cells also needs a way out. Much like the household trash, this cellular waste must be taken out on a regular basis.

How do you know if you have cellular toxins? We all do. We are exposed to millions of them. In fact, more than 65,000 new chemicals have been introduced into the environment since 1950.[1] Over time, our body becomes overloaded and can't keep up with the daily onslaught. Signs of toxin overload can include lack of energy, weight problems, poor digestion, weakened immune system, headaches, and an overall lack of vitality – all of which can lead to stress.

If your body is full of toxins, your bodily systems are in constant crisis mode. Toxins from processed food, polluted water, plastics, and commercial produce can create a response in your body akin to a low-grade infection. It takes tremendous energy for a body to continually fight an infection. Getting rid of some of these accumulated toxins can free up massive amounts of energy.

You'll feel better, look better, and sleep better. When you lighten your cellular load, you'll also be better equipped to handle your to-do list, gracefully respond to life's challenges, and balance the demands of work and home life.

So how do toxins get into your body in the first place? Three ways:

- You eat them

- You breathe them

- You put them on your body

Once the toxins are in there, how do you get them out?

Fortunately, your body has four methods or "exit paths" for naturally removing toxins:

- Exit path # 1 → from the colon via poop

- Exit path # 2 → from the kidneys via pee

- Exit path # 3 → from the skin in the form of sweat

- Exit path # 4 → from the lungs in the form of breath

The good news is there is a lot you can do to assist these four methods of toxin removal. The first eight techniques in **Lighten Your Load** will show you how to get existing toxins out of your body.

1. DRINK ENOUGH WATER

"Drinking water is like washing out your insides. The water will cleanse the system, fill you up, decrease your caloric load, and improve the function of all your tissues."
– **Kevin R. Stone**, M.D.

There are three things to know about water to lighten your toxic load:

- How much to drink

- When to drink it

- Why it's important

Let's start at the top. We all know that we need to drink plenty of water each day. But how much is enough?

The ideal amount varies from person to person, but as a general rule, if you're not going to the bathroom approximately once per hour, you're not drinking enough. If your urine is darker than a pale yellow color, you're not drinking enough.

A common formula for determining how much water to drink is to take your body weight in pounds and divide that number by two. The resulting number is the number of ounces you need to drink each day. So if you weigh 144 pounds, dividing 144 by two gives you 72 ounces, which equals nine 8-ounce glasses of water a day. Simple!

But that's just a baseline. If you drink a cup of coffee or a glass of wine, you'll need to add another glass of water to balance it out because beverages containing alcohol or caffeine are dehydrating.

So now that we know how much to drink, it's equally important to know *when* to drink it.

Most people go hours at a time without drinking water and then guzzle down a glass or two randomly. As a result, most of us are chronically dehydrated. Dehydration leads to inflammation, inflammation then leads to pain, pain leads to illness…you get the idea. So what's a better way?

Drink a large glass of water first thing in the morning and then sip water throughout the day.

By sipping water throughout the day, your body learns that water is always available, so it will perform all of its functions more efficiently.

Now comes the *why*.

The obvious reason to drink more water is that more water = more pee = more toxins that can be flushed from your system. Not so obvious, perhaps, is the link between dehydration and stress.

Your body is roughly 60-65 percent water. Your brain, though, is closer to 75 percent water. Your brain needs water to produce hormones and neurotransmitters so the rest of your body can function properly and generate new cells.

Bottom line: without enough water, your body and mind cannot function optimally. End result? Mental fogginess, low energy, and stress.

Stress, in turn, causes more dehydration.

According to College of Natural Nutrition founder Barbara Wren, "Any kind of stress is registered on the water component of the body as dehydration. As soon as the body is dehydrated, it is expressed as stress. So external stress causes cellular dehydration, which then causes internal stress."[2] This creates a cycle within the body. Stress leads to dehydration, and dehydration leads to more stress.

For years, and occasionally even now, I struggled with the whole water issue. Either I didn't feel like drinking anything or I was too lazy to go downstairs to get a glass of water. I rarely felt thirsty. Red alert! It turns out that having no energy, feeling lethargic or moody, and *not feeling thirsty* are actually three signs of dehydration! Other signs of dehydration include headaches, muscle cramps, and food cravings. Food cravings, especially sweets, add to the overall toxic load of the body.

The key to drinking more water is to surround yourself with it. Make it easy on yourself. Keep a full glass of water on your bedside table so you can take a sip before bed and finish the rest in the morning. Keep another full glass on your desk at work. Carry some water with you wherever you go.

LIGHTEN YOUR LOAD NOW

- Calculate the number of ounces of water your body needs per day by dividing your body weight (in pounds) in half.

- Drink a large glass of water first thing in the morning and then sip water throughout the day.

- Check the color of your urine throughout the day and adjust your water intake accordingly.

2. ADD LEMON FOR YOUR LIVER

It's easier to drink more water when you jazz it up. Try adding a sprig of mint or a slice of cucumber to your glass of water. For the most bang for your detox buck, add some lemon. Here's why:

Lemon is good for your liver. A healthy liver is critical for daily detoxification. As your body's largest internal organ, the liver plays a major role in purifying the blood and eliminating toxins and waste.

Lemons have powerful cleansing and detoxification properties. They are one of the only foods that produce bile similar to what the liver produces. So by adding more lemon to your diet, you are giving your liver a break. Other benefits of lemon include:

- Jumpstarts the digestive system

- Helps with indigestion and constipation

- Supports weight loss

- Helps balance pH levels. Although lemon is acidic in taste, it has an alkalinizing effect on the body.

- Contains antioxidants which can help flush out toxins and free radicals

- Helps maintain your immune system

Need one more reason to add some lemon to your water? Your skin will thank you. Anything that benefits the liver can have a positive effect on the skin as well since the two are directly related. The anti-aging properties in lemon juice can help prevent wrinkles and acne.

LIGHTEN YOUR LOAD NOW

- Add half of a freshly squeezed organic lemon to an eight-ounce glass of purified water. Room-temperature (or warmer) water is preferred as warmer water helps stimulate digestion and takes less energy for the body to assimilate.

- Add fresh mint, cucumber, or ginger for variety and an extra detox kick.

3. CLEANSE

Would you go for a month or two without taking a shower? How about six months without washing your clothes or cleaning your house? Unthinkable, right? Yet most of us go years – even decades – without cleaning the *inside* of our bodies. Most people have hundreds of foreign compounds in their bodies. It's a good idea to clean them out regularly.

You might be surprised to know that the average person is carrying around a good 4-15 pounds (2-7 kilograms) of waste matter compacted on the colon wall. It's not just food waste – it's also mucus from your cells and tissues. The mucus develops to protect your stomach and colon from the festering offenders.

Ideally the body takes care of daily detoxification in the form of a bowel movement after every meal. The reality is that most of us don't experience such frequent movement. Dehydration is one reason. Not enough fiber and too much processed food in our diet is another. Eating too much too late at night can also be a contributor.

Cleansing can be a powerful way to tackle accumulated toxins, waste, and mucus and remove them from the body through the colon. But it's not just the colon that needs cleansing. Cleaning the liver, kidneys, and bladder is equally important since not all toxins make it to the colon.

There are several methods for cleansing:

- Three- or five-day green juice cleanses. Giving your body a break from solid foods can free up energy for deeper detoxification. Unfortunately, you're not fundamentally changing how you eat once the three days are up, so the toxins will start to accumulate once again.

- Colon hydrotherapy, otherwise known as colonics. This is a fast and effective way to clean up waste, but a series of sessions can be a bit pricey.

- Group nutritional cleanse programs. Programs that teach you which foods are toxic triggers for your individual body offer more long-term, lasting results since you are taking the toxins out while simultaneously reducing the amount of incoming offenders, ideally forever. Full disclosure, I offer an "Ultimate Life and Body Reboot" program that includes a cleanse, so I am partial to this route.

Most cleanse programs aim to give your digestive system a break – by eating much less (or not at all) – so it can unload the toxin buildup in your colon, liver, cells, and tissues.

Be sure to check with your doctor or healthcare professional before embarking on any cleanse or detoxification program.

LIGHTEN YOUR LOAD NOW

- Add more clean water and fiber to your diet.
- Consider a group cleanse program for more hands-on support.

4. BRUSH YOUR SKIN

Your skin is your largest organ. It is a protective barrier that shields you from environmental pollutants. However, if your pores are clogged, you are trapping waste and dead skin cells inside. Yuck! Studies have shown that an entire pound of waste is eliminated by the skin each day. Dry skin brushing can help to move things along and allow your skin to breathe.

Skin brushing stimulates the lymphatic system and helps get rid of unwanted materials and toxins in the body. It can even help reduce cellulite.[3] What more could you want? It's cheap, easy, and effective.

Skin brushes are not the same as a loofah. Your skin must be dry to properly brush it.

Here's how to use a skin brush: Start at your feet and brush up from there toward your heart. Avoid your face, but spend a good 15 minutes brushing everything else. It's that simple! If you don't already have a skin brush, it is best to choose one made from all natural fibers such as bamboo or tampico.

Consistency is key. Try it for 15 minutes per day. In a month you will likely see and feel the difference!

LIGHTEN YOUR LOAD NOW

- Visit your local health food store and invest in a skin brush made from natural fibers. Most cost under $20 US.

5. SWEAT

Now that your pores are unclogged from skin brushing, it's easier to sweat out some of those toxins. Sweating is healthy and important for detox. Unfortunately, we often block this natural bodily function. We wear synthetic fabrics that don't allow the skin to breathe. We use deodorant that contains chemicals so our armpits don't sweat, which is a double whammy since you are introducing a toxin while blocking the release of others. In addition, many of us live sedentary lives where working up a vigorous sweat is not part of our daily routine.

There are many ways to counter this. Here are a few of them:

Cardio Exercise

We've known for years that aerobic exercise is important to boost your metabolism, reduce body fat, and keep your heart healthy. What you may not realize is that cardio exercise has significant detox benefits. Aside from the benefits of sweating, cardio exercise also stimulates the lymphatic system.

The lymphatic system, which includes your lymph nodes, spleen, tonsils, and thymus gland, is much like a sewer system for the body. It carries cellular waste from the tissues to the bloodstream, where it can then make its way to the body's main detoxification organs: the liver and kidneys. Unlike the body's circulatory system, which has the heart to keep the blood moving, the lymphatic system has no pump. That means it's up to us to get the lymph moving. This movement is important, as your body contains three times more lymph than blood!

You don't need a treadmill, elliptical machine, or even a spare hour in the day to get enough cardio to make a difference. For a quick cardio blast, try jumping. Jumping rope is not just for kids! It's one of the fastest ways to get your heart pumping. In fact, you don't even need the rope. Just jump up and down to one of your favorite upbeat songs. Start with a short 2- to 3-minute song and see if you can keep jumping to the end. Then gradually work up to a longer song. Experts say 10 minutes of jumping yields the same cardiovascular benefits as 30 minutes of running.[4] For best results, wear tennis shoes and jump on a semi-soft surface. Avoid jumping barefoot on tile or concrete.

Epsom Salt Bath

While soaking in a hot bath will make you sweat, adding Epsom salt to the bath will facilitate detoxification through the skin. The physical and mental benefits of Epsom salt have been known for hundreds of years. On the physical side, Epsom salt (magnesium sulfate) draws toxins and heavy metals out of the body while replenishing the level of magnesium in the body. Magnesium helps to produce serotonin, which in turn helps boost your mood, your energy level, and your overall sense of calm. You can detox and de-stress at the same time!

Consider taking an Epsom salt bath once or twice per week. Add two cups (approximately 500 grams) of salt in each bath and soak for about 20 minutes. Make sure your bath water is filtered, otherwise you are introducing chlorine and other pollutants into your body at the same time. It is best also to avoid the fancy brands of Epsom salt with added artificial perfumes or the catchall term "fragrance." You can buy Epsom salt in bulk from most gardening centers and pharmacies.

Other Sweaty Endeavors

Float tanks and far infrared saunas are also great for releasing toxins through the skin. Float tanks are like an Epsom salt bath on steroids. Instead of two cups of salt in your bath, imagine a thousand pounds of salt – so much salt that your body floats effortlessly in the water.

Far infrared saunas allow the body to sweat at lower temperatures than would be possible in a conventional sauna. In an infrared sauna, approximately 20 percent of the energy is used to heat the air, leaving the remaining 80 percent to heat the body.

Be sure to consult with your doctor or healthcare professional before embarking on a new exercise program or using a float tank or far infrared sauna.

LIGHTEN YOUR LOAD NOW

- Pick one new sweaty action to incorporate this week.

- Let your skin breathe while you sleep. Replace your synthetic nightgown or nightshirt with an organic cotton alternative (or if you sleep *au naturel* use organic cotton sheets).

6. BREATHE DEEPLY

"Once we reconnect with our breath, we are able to access our deeper knowing and break free of vicious cycles of anxiety."
— **Sonia Choquette,** author of *Tune In*

If you were going to pick just one way to **Lighten Your Load**, this would be it. In fact, I had a hard time deciding which chapter to put this technique in because breathing deeply and consciously can be a life-changer in releasing physical, mental, and emotional toxins and stress. Conscious and deep breathing helps detox your body, unclutter your mind, and promote an overall sense of calm, peace, and well-being.

What does breathing have to do with releasing physical toxins? Everything! Deep breathing clears the lungs, brings vital oxygen to your cells, stimulates the lymph, and releases toxins when you exhale. In fact, it is estimated that half of our body's toxins can be eliminated through deep exhalation.

The problem is that most of us don't breathe properly. Our breaths are shallow and quick. If we do take the occasional deep breath, we do so from the chest up – our chest expands, our shoulders rise toward our ears, and our heads fill with air. Not ideal.

When your breath is quick and shallow, your body's cleansing and detoxifying systems cannot work at full capacity.

Proper deep breathing comes from the belly. Try it now. As you inhale, let your belly expand. As you exhale, draw in your belly. This may take some practice getting used to, especially if you're used to sucking in your abs all the time. So for your next deep breath, let those abs relax. Also be sure to keep your spine straight and your shoulders relaxed.

If you still find it challenging to let the belly expand on the inhale, practice belly breathing while lying down. Place your hands on your abdomen and feel it rise and fall as you breathe deeply.

Let's practice. Take a couple of deep breaths right now.

Great. Now that you know *how* to do it, the next question is *when* to do it. After all, breathing is an unconscious activity. It happens automatically on its own, without our having to think about it.

The trick is to start thinking about it and practice breathing *consciously* as often as you can.

This might sound a bit "out there," but the simple practice of breathing consciously can transform your life. I'm serious. If you could learn and incorporate only one thing from this book, I would recommend this: breathe deeply and consciously as often as possible. Many times a day. Here's why:

Focusing on your breathing forces you to be present in the moment, which means you *automatically calm your mind* and quiet the negative or fearful looping thoughts that add to your stress level. Not only is conscious breathing the fastest and most effective way to calm your mind and detox your body, it's also simple and free. It sounds so easy!

Unfortunately, most of us have never been taught how to be present in the moment. We have decades of experience in NOT consciously using our breath. We are trained since childhood to use our minds for everything. We've become good at reacting to life and mentally trying to figure things out. Years ago, if someone were to tell me to "take a deep breath" when I was in the midst of a crisis, I would have thought it to be unhelpful, "woo woo" advice. How could a deep breath or two solve my problem? Turns out it does.

Conscious, deep breathing = fewer physical and mental toxins = more energy and less stress = you feel better. If you calm the mind and detox the body, you will naturally sleep better as well. The best part about conscious breathing is that you can do it on your own. There's no need to set aside an hour to focus on breathing. Just start with this moment.

Take another deep, conscious breath right now. Feel your belly expand on the inhale. Notice the belly relaxing on the exhale.

Excellent!

Now that we've covered how, when, and why to take deep, conscious breaths, the trick is to actually do it. This takes practice. Chances are good that you are not used to thinking about breathing, so even if you decide right now to add a few deep breaths to your day, it might not happen. I know this from years of personal experience.

The key to successfully incorporating deep, conscious breathing into your day is to link it with an activity you are already doing. Here are some examples:

- In the shower: Every time you have a shower, take a few deep breaths. Enjoy the hot water falling onto your skin. Feel gratitude for all the good in your life.

- At meals: Take a few deep breaths of thanks before every meal.

- In the car: As soon as you get into your car, take 30 seconds to close your eyes and breathe. Do the same before you get out of the car.

- At work: Take one deep, cleansing breath in between each major task, phone call, or meeting.

- At the carpool: When picking up the kids from school, consider arriving a few minutes early to just sit, breathe deeply, and enjoy the silence.

- In the bathroom: Use this time to close your eyes, center yourself, and breathe consciously (you may want to skip the very deep breathing if you're in a public WC!).

LIGHTEN YOUR LOAD NOW

- Choose one creative way to add a few conscious breaths to your daily routine.

7. OPEN THE WINDOWS

It stands to reason that if you can release roughly 50 percent of your body's toxins through deep exhalations, then what you breathe *in* on a daily basis can add significantly to your toxic load.

Adults take about 25,000 breaths per day. What are you inhaling with each of those breaths?

Consider how much time you spend at home or at the office. You might be surprised at just how much time you spend indoors. According to the Environmental Protection Agency, the average American spends 87 percent of her life indoors. Not good.

The quality of the air you breathe inside your home and office is often more polluted than the air outdoors. In fact, the indoor air you breathe could be 5-10 times more polluted than outdoor air. Why is this? These are just some of the common indoor toxic offenders:

- Chemical household cleaners

- Pet dander

- Finishing agents on furniture

- Mold and mildew

- Dust mites

- Outgassing from volatile organic compounds such as formaldehyde, which is used in carpet, furniture, and even bed linens!

- Candles

- Synthetic air fresheners

- Paint and other stored chemicals

- Even your own exhaled breaths add to the toxic mix indoors. So open the windows and let the fresh air in!

LIGHTEN YOUR LOAD NOW

- Open the windows, especially when cooking, cleaning, or using paint or other chemical-based hobby supplies. Consider using a portable fan as well to pull the air out of the room.

8. MOVE YOUR BODY

This is a big one. I already mentioned cardio exercise as a great way to sweat out toxins. Although an hour of cardio a day would be nice, it's not realistic or fun for many of us. In this *Lighten Your Load* strategy, I'm referring to more general, everyday types of movement.

Newsflash: Your body is designed to be moved IN ALL DIREC-TIONS every day. Think about that for a second. Have you had to really reach up for something today, perhaps getting something off the top shelf of the cabinet? Have you arched your back and stretched your arms out to the sides? What about twisting side to side from the waist? How about a diagonal stretch – where you reach an arm over your head and toward the opposite corner of the ceiling?

Chances are, the most common direction your body has moved today is in forward flexion, otherwise known as hunching forward. For many of us, we spend at least one-third of our day this way, either sitting hunched over at our desks or driving hunched over behind the wheel of the car. Over time, this hunching habit creeps into other areas.

Take a look around. Watch people as they walk. Are their shoulders rolled forward? Are their heads thrust forward and down? Even if they're not texting while they're walking, the answer is likely yes.

When we don't fully move our bodies as nature intended, things get stuck. You might be constipated, which means trapped physical toxins. You might notice stiff joints or an aching lower back.

An inflexible body leads to an inflexible mind, and vice versa. That's why movement is so important. Movement plays a critical role in releasing physical, mental, and emotional toxins.

Movement through exercise changes your brain chemistry, boosts your mood, and allows you to focus, giving you more time in your day. You don't need to run ten miles a day or join a cardio kickboxing class. Even five minutes of movement sprinkled throughout your day will do wonders. You will think more clearly. You'll sleep better. You'll feel better.

Here are some five-minute movement ideas to get you started:

- Take a brisk walk around the block. It gives you an immediate energy and mood boost.

- Use the stairs instead of the elevator.

- Wherever you drive, park in a space far from the entrance.

- When grocery shopping, take the shopping cart back inside the store rather than leaving it in the parking lot.

- Dance to one of your favorite tunes. I'm partial to salsa dancing, but any type of upbeat music will do!

- Jump in place. No rope needed.

Perhaps you already work out regularly and practice many of the above suggestions. Want to take it to the next level? Try mindful movement. In mindful movement, you bring conscious awareness and conscious breathing into each move. When stretching or walking, for example, pay attention to how your body feels and moves. Listen to your body. Rather than thinking about your work project or your weekend plans, bring all of your attention *inside* the body. Notice any sensations or tension. Become aware of your breath. As you exhale, visualize the tension exiting the body.

Mindful movement can do wonders for reducing emotional toxins, such as repressed anger, frustration, and sadness. These emotions need a way out as well. If you don't let them out, they can become stuck and buried within and will eventually find their way out in the form of something seemingly unrelated like an accident, illness, or addiction.

Try these movement methods for releasing unwanted emotional energy and toxins:

- Literally shake off the negative energy of others by jumping and flailing around wildly. For better results, move wildly in front of a mirror as you make faces at yourself. You are guaranteed to crack yourself up, and laughter just happens to have tremendous detox benefits!

- Release anger by beating up a pillow.

- Try mindful movement practices such as stretching, yoga, Pilates, Tai Chi, and Qigong. As always, check with your doctor or healthcare professional before beginning any exercise program. You are the expert on you.

LIGHTEN YOUR LOAD NOW

- Start by incorporating one five-minute movement break into each day this week, and then increase it to two next week, and so on.

- Shake your body and let emotions out.

CHAPTER SUMMARY

In this chapter, you lightened your load of cellular toxins using the four "exit paths" of pee, poop, sweat, and breath. We also identified eight ways to reduce the amount of waste and other gunk that is already in your body:

- Drink enough water

- Add lemon for your liver

- Cleanse

- Brush your skin

- Sweat

- Breathe deeply

- Open the windows

- Move your body

In the next chapter, you'll lighten your physical load.

4 | LIGHTEN YOUR PHYSICAL LOAD

Physical toxins. You eat them, drink them, wear them, and slather them on your skin. In contrast to cellular toxins, which are already in your body, physical toxins are those you actively put in and on your body. Of course, it's not just you. Everyone in the modern, industrialized world does this, perhaps without realizing the consequences.

The next four ways to *Lighten Your Load* will show you how to reduce the amount of new toxins coming in.

9. UPGRADE YOUR WATER

All water is not considered equal. There's municipal tap water, filtered water, distilled water, well water, spring water – the list can go on and on.

In Chapter Three, you discovered how much water your body needs and when it's best to drink it. In this strategy to *Lighten Your Load,* we look at the quality of the water you're pouring into your body.

Take a moment to consider the type of water you use on a daily basis:

- What type of water do you drink at home?

- What is your water source at the office?

- When dining out, do you ask whether the water has been filtered or purified?

- How much of the water you drink comes out of plastic bottles?

As we saw earlier, drinking plenty of water helps remove toxins and waste products. However, your body cannot properly remove toxins if the water you are drinking is toxic to begin with. Upgrading the water you drink (and the container you put it in) can dramatically reduce the amount of toxins you take in.

The first step to upgrade your drinking water is to avoid the worst water source – and that's unfiltered tap water. Here's why:

Tap water is contaminated. It contains chlorine, fluoride, mercury, heavy metals, and prescription drug residues. A 2009 report by the Environmental Working Group found more than 300 contaminants in 20 million tap water quality tests, which were conducted at utilities that supply water to 231 million people.[1] Yikes!

Simply avoiding tap water at home, in the office, and at restaurants can dramatically reduce the toxins you consume.

The next step would be to minimize the amount of water you ingest that comes from plastic bottles. There are two main reasons for this: 1) plastics expose you to a whole other category of toxins called xeno-estrogens, and 2) plastics place an extraordinary toxic load on the planet.

Let's explore both of these.

Plastics in Your Body

Research suggests that most plastic leaches chemicals when heated. The plastic water bottle you're drinking out of was likely heated several times before you drank out of it. Consider this common scenario:

- Pallets of bottled water are delivered to supermarkets *in unrefrigerated trucks*. Depending on the distance traveled and the season of the year, the temperature of those bottles can vary widely in transit.

- The water cools down to room temperature while it's out on the store floor.

- You purchase a case of this water and put it in the back of your car, where the plastic heats up again.

- You store the case of water in the garage, subjecting it to more temperature fluctuations.

- You then place some of it in the refrigerator, freezer, or ice chest to cool it down.

- You grab a water bottle as you go out to run errands.

- You leave it in the car while you're in the store.

- Eventually you drink it, after that plastic has been heated and cooled a half-dozen times.

Chemicals that leach out of heated plastic, particularly BPA, have been shown to mimic estrogen in the body.[2] These hormone-like chemicals are referred to as "xeno-estrogens" or simply "bad estrogens." They have been linked to a number of health challenges. Best to avoid them.

Plastics in the Environment

Plastics put a heavy toxic load on the planet. According to the Earth Policy Institute, in 1976, Americans drank an average of 1.6 gallons of bottled water every year. Today it is well over 30 gallons per person per year.[3] The production of plastic bottles requires millions of barrels of oil each year. The amount of crude oil used to make just one year's supply of empty water bottles would fuel 100,000 cars for a year. *National Geographic* calculates this to be more than 17 million barrels of oil annually, which is equivalent to 2.5 million tons of carbon dioxide released into the atmosphere.[4] Even more oil is used for the fuel to haul bottled water to consumers all over the world, which means thousands of tons of additional carbon dioxide in the atmosphere for us to breathe in daily.

Disposal of plastic waste is another problem. According to the Container Recycling Institute, EACH DAY in the U.S. more than 60 MILLION water bottles are thrown away.[5] Visualize that for a moment. Only about 13 percent are recycled. Some 40 billion bottles a year (that's billions with a "b") end up in landfills where they can take up to 1,000 years to biodegrade. Others are incinerated, releasing toxic by-products such as chlorine gas and ash containing heavy metals into the air. And many of the rest end up in the ocean. In fact, there is an area of floating plastic trash in the Northern Pacific Ocean that's twice the size of the state of Texas. Described as the "biggest trash dump in the world," much of it consists of plastic bottles.

LIGHTEN YOUR LOAD NOW

- Avoid tap water. Upgrade to filtered water, or even better, natural spring water.

- Skip the plastic and opt for water bottled in glass, metal, or ceramic whenever possible.

10. GET A SHOWER FILTER

If tap water is not fit to drink, bathing in it might not be the best idea either. The reason? Chlorine. You might be surprised to know that one hot shower is equivalent to drinking seven glasses of tap water!

While our skin acts as a barrier to many pollutants, stuff still gets in. That's why many prescription drugs are now available in patches. We stick them on our skin, and the stuff gets absorbed directly into our bloodstream.

The chlorine in tap water gets absorbed by our skin just as the prescription medications. Some suggest that we actually absorb more chlorine by bathing in it than we do by drinking it because when we drink, our body is able to filter out some of it in the liver before it enters the bloodstream, whereas with bathing, it gets absorbed directly.

In addition, we breathe chlorine into our lungs when we bathe in it.

Of course, there are some benefits of chlorine, which is why it is in the tap water in the first place. Chlorine kills unwanted organisms and bacteria. But it can also kill the healthy, defensive bacteria we have on and in our body. Best to avoid it.

LIGHTEN YOUR LOAD NOW

- Get a shower filter.

11. EAT YOUR L'S

You can lighten the toxic load from the food you eat by opting for what I call the 3 L's, that is, Local, Live, and Light.

Local

Local produce has more nutrients. Why? Three reasons:

- It's picked when it's ripe.
- It's fresh.
- It's likely organic.

Eating local means you're not eating something that was picked a week or two ago when it wasn't fully ripe. Produce that is shipped across the country – or across the world – is often irradiated (which "nukes" nutrients along with unwanted critters) or waxed (to make it appear fresher). Local farmers are less likely to use pesticides and other chemicals, even if they are certified organic.

Live

Consider this: We are the only species on the planet that cooks their food. We are also the only species on the planet that nukes it. Cooking food destroys some of the nutrients and enzymes needed to digest the food. Microwaving kills most of them. The more food is processed or cooked, the fewer nutrients it has left in it by the time you eat it.

When your body doesn't get the nutrients it needs, you will feel hungry. You will likely eat more.

Light

Food for thought: We are also the only species that eats when we are not hungry. Can you imagine a lion eating because he's had a bad day? Or a bird mindlessly eating long after it's full? It doesn't happen. We are the only ones who eat for emotional reasons.

When you are stressed out, overscheduled, or angry, do you reach for that bright, shiny apple? Probably not. If you are like most people, when your emotions pick the snack, it's likely to be a heavy one, dense and packed with anything but vital nutrients. This type of food literally weighs you down, clouds your thinking, and adds to the stress load you were trying to escape by eating it. Not good.

Eating light means two things: 1) eating a bit less than you normally would, and 2) eating foods that are as close to the original source as possible.

Digestion uses an enormous amount of energy. If you practice eating just a bit less at each meal, your body will quickly adjust. You will likely feel lighter, have more energy, and as longevity experts suggest, you will live longer as a result.

In addition, foods that are closest to their original source, such as raw foods and unprocessed foods, are literally lighter. They have a higher energetic frequency than do their processed, cooked, or microwaved counterparts. They have a lighter effect on the body. You need less of them to satisfy your hunger. They take less energy to digest, which means more of your energy is available for other things, be it deeper detoxification or keeping up with the kids.

Of course, when in doubt, consult with a qualified nutritionist or dietician to determine what's best for your body.

LIGHTEN YOUR LOAD NOW

- The next time you shop, go local! Visit a farmers' market or local farm. Trade that prepackaged lunch or fast food for local or organic alternatives. Your body and mind will thank you!

- Begin to wean yourself from your microwave. See how long you can go without using it.

12. GO NATURAL

Don't worry, you don't need to stop using deodorant or shaving your legs. But you may want to reconsider the products you regularly slather on your body.

A good rule of thumb is "if you wouldn't eat it, best not to put in on your body." Why? Because as we discovered with chlorine in your shower water, absorbing chemicals through your skin is equivalent (and sometimes worse) than if you were to eat them directly.

Take a look at the labels of some of your personal care products, such as shampoo, lotion, hairspray, soap, and anything else you apply to your body. Do you know what all the ingredients are? Do you know what even *half* of them are?

The next time you shop for these items, consider buying a more natural alternative. Don't be fooled by terms such as "all natural" and "organic" when it comes to cosmetics and body products. Phrases like "active ingredients," "key ingredients," and "natural" are often used to distract us from investigating the small print of what is really in the product.

The clothes we wear, the towels we use, and the sheets we sleep on can also be a source of unwanted toxins. Most synthetic fabrics such as rayon, polyester, acrylic, and spandex are treated with chemicals during and after processing. Many of these cannot be washed out. This is especially true for clothes that claim to be "wrinkle-free," "shrink-resistant," or "waterproof." Buyer beware.

LIGHTEN YOUR LOAD NOW

- The next time you run out of a personal care item like toothpaste, body lotion, or shampoo, upgrade to a more natural alternative.

- For your next clothing purchase, consider 100 percent organic, natural fabrics from cotton, bamboo, hemp, flax, or linen.

Breathing Check-in

Before moving on, let's revisit strategy # 6: Breathe deeply.

Did you choose a creative way to add a few conscious breaths to your daily routine? Perhaps you came up with a word or action to remind yourself to stop, breathe, and center yourself?

Let's take a moment right now to do it.

Ready?

OK, go.

Did you do it?

Seriously, go ahead and take a moment now. It doesn't matter if you are at the office. Just relax and follow your breath a few times.

Ahhhh, that's better, isn't it?

You can cleanse your mind and detox your body by spending just ONE minute, several times a day, with your breathing. Don't get discouraged if you forget. Sometimes it can take patience and perseverance to make a positive, life-changing habit really stick!

OK, moving on…

5 | LIGHTEN YOUR LOAD OF STUFF

More stuff = more stress.

It's that simple.

We often don't make the connection between our cluttered, stuffed homes and our scattered, cluttered minds.

But there is, indeed, a connection.

It's hard to feel peaceful and focused when your desk is cluttered with piles of paper or your car is full of stuff. Physical clutter takes a mental toll. Cluttered space = cluttered mind. Excess stuff wears you down.

Think of one area in your home or office that needs cleaning up and clearing out. It doesn't matter how big or small it is. Maybe it's a closet, drawer, or section of your desk you've been "meaning to get to." How do you feel when you walk by that area, day after day? Every time you look at it, you are reminded of what hasn't been done.

Here's the thing about stuff. More stuff doesn't make you happier. Just look around you. If you're like most people, you don't use even half of the stuff you own. Think of the 80/20 rule. People spend 80 percent of their time in just 20 percent of their living space. You likely use only about 20 percent of all the stuff in your home on a regular basis. The rest just sits there. It gathers dust. It takes up space. Not just physical space. Your physical stuff takes up mental and emotional space as well.

In this chapter, I invite you to take a good look at your stuff and how it might be adding to your stress load. We'll then look at six ways to declutter, organize, and simplify your stuff.

Before we get to the specific strategies, it's worth exploring why we have all this stuff in the first place. In the Western world, and particularly in the United States, we are conditioned to believe "more is better" practically from the moment we are born. We are bombarded daily by thousands of media messages that reinforce this belief. The underlying message in nearly all mainstream media – including TV, radio, magazines, and newspapers – is that there's something wrong with you, and the solution is to buy something, whether it's another beauty cream, a bigger car, or the latest electronic gadget.

We grow up in a rat race for more, and we assume that, at some point, all that "more" will result in happiness. It doesn't. There's a reason it's called a "rat race." It goes against human nature.

Our human nature is as human BEings, not human DOings or human HAVEings. BEing refers to natural internal states like peace, balance, and joy, none of which can be purchased with external stuff. The fast track to inner peace and joy is not via buying more, having more, or doing more. These internal states are experienced when we actively make space for them.

Decluttering and simplifying your stuff are two such ways to make space so you can have more of what you *really* want in life – greater fun, joy, love, ease, growth, connection, freedom, adventure, and purpose.

Don't worry, you won't have to become a minimalist to reap the benefits of simplifying. In fact, you can be a minimalist and still be stressed out and toxic.

It is helpful, however, to realize WHY you buy things. Is it a need or a want? There's nothing wrong with wanting things, but *why* do you want them? What is the emotion or unmet need behind it? Most of what we buy is based on emotion. The same is true of what we eat. Many of us eat for emotional reasons or as a way to "stuff" our feelings. We often do the same with physical stuff in our homes.

As you experiment with the next six strategies, notice if you become anxious about paring down or throwing something out. Consider the possible mental and emotional reasons behind it. What might you be holding onto in other areas of your life? What might you be trying to stuff down, fill up, avoid, or cover up with all this physical stuff?

Simplicity, which includes simplifying your stuff, is one of the keys to true happiness. Simplifying your life is about more than just cleaning out your closet and getting rid of physical clutter. Simplicity is a fundamental principle for living a life of meaning and joy. Just let that idea float around in your mind as we explore these next six ways to *Lighten Your Load.*

13. CLEAR YOUR CLUTTER

Take a look at your desk or your kitchen counter. Is it organized and spacious, or can you barely see the surface? The first step to clearing your clutter is to start small.

While it's tempting to begin with the largest area that bugs you the most, that isn't necessarily the best strategy. Remember the last time you decided to tackle your bedroom closet or your entire office? When you start pulling things out of the closet, the entire house can suddenly look like a tornado hit it.

The result?

You're overwhelmed, and that just adds to your stress.

The key to decluttering is to go for the small, immediate win. Here's how:

Look around you. Pick a small area that is messy or cluttered. It could be a corner of your desk, your sock drawer, or a shelf in your medicine cabinet. Ideally, it is something that you look at every day.

Have you picked your area?

Good. Now it's time to dig in. Spread out the items in front of you and take a good look. Ask yourself these questions about each item:

- "Do I actually use this item?" "Have I used it in the last six months?"
    - o If the answer is "No," consider donating or recycling it.

- "Does this item positively contribute to my life?"
    - o If no, consider donating or recycling it.
    - o If yes, dig a little deeper, and ask yourself *how* it adds to your life.

- "Am I keeping this because I think I *might* use it at some point?"
    o   If yes, set it aside for now.

- "Am I keeping it out of guilt?" "Are there items here that I don't actively use and don't really add to my life, but I feel guilty about getting rid of them?"
    o   Oftentimes family heirlooms and gifts from others fall into this category. Consider finding another home for those "guilt" items.

Now look at the items you have set aside because you might use them later. Put these items in a box and mark it with today's date. Put the box somewhere where you won't see it every day. Make a note on your calendar for six months from now to check the box. When you look at the items in that box in six months' time, ask yourself if you missed any of these items. If not, it's time to donate or recycle them.

Put all your donation items in bags and boxes and remove them from sight. Either put them in the car now to take to a donation center or place them in the garage while you arrange for them to be picked up. Don't give your mind an opportunity to dwell on the items. A better approach would be to simply thank each item mentally for whatever joy or utility it brought to you and then mentally release them all to those who will benefit from them even more.

After you've cleaned out the clutter and created some much needed space, the next step is to keep it that way. At the end of each day, double check to be sure that your one tiny area, shelf, or drawer remains spacious and clutter-free. You might be surprised by how that one tiny, clutter-free zone promotes a tremendous feeling of peace, calm, and success!

I know this from personal experience. My nemesis used to be my desk. I typically have 2-3 projects going on simultaneously, and I'm a voracious reader, so my office desk would often overflow with stuff. I used to spread my work projects all around – papers here, stacks of books there, things I wanted to get to eventually – you get the idea. But when I entered my office in the morning and saw all that stuff, I started to feel overwhelmed.

No more! I got rid of the piles and now only keep on my desk what I am currently working on. At the end of each day, I clear off the entire thing and put everything back in its place. What a difference it has made, not only to my productivity but to my stress level as well.

LIGHTEN YOUR LOAD NOW

- Make a list of the 10 areas that could use some decluttering.
- Start with the smallest one first.

14. WEAR IT OR DONATE IT

As we saw with the last strategy, your bedroom closet would not be the first place to start if you want to experience an immediate declutter win. A much more fun way to simplify your wardrobe is the "wear it or donate it" strategy. This strategy consists of three parts.

The first part is to determine which clothing items no longer fit you. Sadly, many women I have worked with have three sets of clothes: 1) the "fat clothes" they used to wear, 2) the "skinny clothes" they hope to get back into, and 3) the clothes they are currently wearing. Why do we do this? It amounts to a form of daily, needless torture that only adds to your mental and emotional stress.

If you have clothes that are too big, congratulations! Donate them immediately. If they are too small, no big deal. While we often think keeping clothes that are too small is an incentive to drop the extra pounds, for most of us, it is counterproductive. Instead, it's really a daily reminder that you are too big for them. Best to get rid of them now and then celebrate your weight loss if and when it happens by buying some new clothes.

Part two of the "Wear it or donate it" strategy is the 12-month rule. Go through your closet again and set aside anything you haven't worn in the last 12 months. Include everything: lingerie, workout clothes, coats, socks, and any special occasion outfits. What are you waiting for? If you need a special occasion to wear some of it, then create one. Live a little! I dare you to wear that luxurious lingerie on a random Tuesday – just because.

Now in part three, the real fun begins. Consider this next part as a game. I've done it several times, and it's hilarious. Here's how it works. Create an empty space at the furthermost end of your closet. Perhaps use an empty hanger or two to separate this area from the rest of your clothes. Tonight, put whatever you're wearing right now at the furthermost end of your closet (or do so after washing it). Each day, pick new items to wear *without repeating any items from yesterday*. That means a different shirt AND different pants, skirt, or jeans.

Each day you will pick all of your clothing from the section you have not yet worn.

Keep doing this until you have cycled through all your pants, skirts, and shorts (depending on which season you are currently in). Only repeat the "bottoms" once you have worn them all once. If you get to an item you are not willing to wear, that's a ripe candidate for the donation pile.

After you have worn about one-third of your wardrobe, you will likely have to get creative with your outfits. Start combining things you normally wouldn't. This exercise forces you to look at your clothes in a refreshing new light. Who knows…you may discover a whole new, more expressive style for yourself.

LIGHTEN YOUR LOAD NOW

- Donate anything that doesn't currently fit you, that you haven't worn in more than 12 months, or that you aren't willing to wear now.

15. NEVER BUY ANOTHER HANGER

If you experimented with the last strategy to *Lighten Your Load,* you likely have several empty hangers in your closet. Wonderful! Now it's time to donate all of those empty hangers – all except three. Keep three empty hangers for future purchases, and challenge yourself to never buy another hanger.

"Now, wait a minute," you might be thinking. "You mean I can only purchase three more items of clothing and then that's it…forever?"

No. That sounds like more stress in the making.

With this strategy, after all your hangers are occupied, when you DO purchase something new, that means you must let go of a clothing item to make room for it. This strategy has the double benefit of making you think twice before buying something new. Is it really something that you will wear often, fits you perfectly, and makes you feel fabulous when you wear it? Do you love it enough to let go of an item you already have?

LIGHTEN YOUR LOAD NOW

> - Keep three empty hangers and donate the rest. Once all hangers are occupied, only purchase a new clothing item when you are prepared to donate another item you already have.

16. LAY IT ALL OUT THERE

When you have had several small victories with strategy # 13, "Clear your clutter," you can move into the bigger areas using the "Lay it all out there" technique. This technique works best for things that are lurking out of sight – behind cabinet doors or inside drawers and closets. Think kitchen cabinets, storage closets, and pantry.

Here's how it works:

- Pick just one of those areas to start with.

- Take everything out of that cabinet or closet and spread it around the room. Depending on how much stuff is in there, you might have to spread it around adjacent rooms as well.

- Now that the cupboard or closet is empty and your stuff is spread all around, only put things back *after* you have actually used them. That's right. Your three different bottle openers, four sets of cloth dinner napkins, and the wok will remain spread out around the house until you use them.

- Once you actually use an item, put it back in the appropriate closet or cupboard. The goal of this exercise is to step back and actually SEE all your stuff. It can be eye-opening for two reasons. On the one hand, just look at all the abundance around you! Take it all in and feel grateful for all the physical abundance you currently enjoy. On the other hand, your eyes might be open-

> Warning! Before you go any further, please realize this is a bold technique, and one that will temporarily make your home or office more cluttered and disorganized.
>
> Another warning! Best to alert your spouse, children, or housemates about your "organization experiment" so they don't wonder why the blender is suddenly in the living room. Remember, you're not actually adding any clutter to your life. You're just bringing all the stuff you already have out of hiding.

ing now to just how many things you have but rarely use. You might also realize that there are thousands of others who would use that stuff more than you.

- If two weeks or a month goes by and you still haven't used your rice cooker or the serving platter you received as a gift from Aunt Bertha, consider passing them on to people who *will* use them.

- Do not feel guilty about donating things you have received as gifts over the years. The act of giving in itself is the gift. What you then do with the gift is nobody's business but yours.

LIGHTEN YOUR LOAD NOW

- Identify a closet or cupboard to start with.
- Schedule a time this week where you can empty it out and spread the contents around the room.

17. SPRING CLEAN YOUR INBOX

Status check:

- How many emails do you receive each day? What about texts?

- Do you get email or text notifications from every social media site you use?

- How many unread email messages do you have in your inbox?

- How many messages are still sitting in your inbox that you have already read?

Much like the desk that was cluttered with stacks of paper and piles of books, an overflowing inbox can become a daily source of anxiety.

Let's give your inbox a good spring cleaning, shall we? Here's how:

- Set aside some time (say, 30 minutes) to do a first pass of your inbox.

- Start with emails that are advertisements and sales offers. Do you buy from these companies on a regular basis? If not, unsubscribe immediately. If yes, just delete them, because they will be sending you more emails soon anyway.

- Next, look at all the e-zines, newsletters, and blogs you subscribe to. Are there 3-4 messages from the same source that you're "saving for later"? Later has arrived! If you're not willing to read them now, best to delete them.

- If you are reluctant to unsubscribe or delete anything, create a new folder and relocate these items there. Schedule a day, one month from now, to go through this folder and read, act on, or delete each item.

LIGHTEN YOUR LOAD NOW

- Start small. Schedule one 30-minute chunk of time when you can tackle your inbox with the delete button. Look for quick and obvious things you can delete or unsubscribe from, such as ads, forwarded chain mail, and old invitations.

18. TOUCH IT ONCE

Now that you have cleaned off your desk and cleared out your email inbox, how do you stop the clutter from creeping back in? How do you stop it from slowly accumulating again?

With the "Touch it once" strategy, you only check your email when you are prepared to act on it, right then. That means you'll need to schedule 1-3 chunks of time per day to engage with your email and resist the urge to check it randomly throughout the day. This technique can be applied to text messages as well.

It's easy to fall into the habit of scrolling through our messages first thing in the morning. We might do this out of curiosity to see what's happening, or it might be a full-on addiction. If you don't have a solid chunk of time in the morning to respond and act upon these messages, looking at them "just to see" is not the best use of your time. The habit of checking email and texts before you leave the house, in the car, while walking, or at other places and times when you *can't do anything about them* puts you in react mode or busyness mode. Both will add to your stress level.

I've had lots of experience with this one. I used to wake up in the morning and check email messages first thing. Even though I knew I wouldn't be able to take action on any of them for several hours, I still felt the need to check them "just in case." As high-performance expert Brendon Burchard likes to say, your email inbox is really just a convenient filing system for other people's agendas. By scheduling specific times for email, you'll have more control over your time and your daily agenda, which can then do wonders for reducing your stress level.

With the "Touch it once" strategy, when you do sit down to go through email, the goal is to interact with the email only once. Here are some examples:

- Is it an "FYI" or "CC" message? Then read it, make a note of whatever is important, and then delete it.

- Does the email require a response or some other action on your part? If time permits, take the action or write the response now. Otherwise, add it to your calendar.

The same can be done with physical "snail" mail. When you pick up the mail, immediately separate the junk mail from the legitimate mail. I personally like to do this as I am walking back to the house. The junk mail rarely makes it indoors; instead, it goes directly into the outside recycle bin.

When indoors, rather than opening everything just to see what's inside, consider waiting until you have a block of time to read and take action.

LIGHTEN YOUR LOAD NOW

- Only check your email when you are prepared to act on it, right then.
- Same goes with snail mail.

CHAPTER SUMMARY

So far, you've lightened your load from some cellular toxins that had accumulated in your body, and you've reduced physical toxins in what you eat, drink, and apply to your skin. You've also simplified your stuff, creating some much needed space for what you really want in life.

In the next chapter, we turn to the last major source of stress – your mental and emotional toxins and clutter.

6 | LIGHTEN YOUR STRESS LOAD

*"Your mind stands for **M**anufacturer of Incessant, Neurotic **D**rama."*
– Karin Kiser

Let's face it – our minds love drama. All it takes is a single thought, and we can easily get swept away on the negativity train.

M I N D also stands for **M**aker-upper of **I**rrational, **N**egative **D**elusions.

Now, don't get me wrong. When used properly, the mind can be a wonderful tool. It's great for data retrieval, planning, and recognizing patterns. As spiritual teacher Osho says, "The mind is a mechanism. It is not you. It records things from outside, and then reacts to outside situations according to those recordings."[1] But more often than not, our mind is more than just a tool. It's actually running our lives!

In this chapter, we explore how our minds and emotions contribute to our stress level. I call these "mental and emotional toxins," and they can include anything from negativity, anger, frustration, and worry to the things we read, the programs we watch, and the people we surround ourselves with.

There is a physical connection as well. Mental and emotional stress plays a HUGE role in our overall health and wellness. Work pressures, family dynamics, relationships, and financial concerns all create stress on the body. Stress can keep those unwanted pounds firmly in place. Emotions such as fear, anger, resentment, and jealousy affect our heart rate, breathing, and blood pressure. Stress can also deplete the body's reserve of nutrients.

So how can you get these mental and emotional toxins out of the body?

Unfortunately, pee and poop aren't as effective here, but there are plenty of other ways to declutter your mind. The most obvious one is to stop feeding it garbage. Complaints, negative self-talk, disempowering thoughts, judgment, and other forms of self-abuse are just some of the ways we add to our mental and emotional stress.

You'll discover how to **Lighten Your Load** of mental and emotional stress with the next 15 strategies. The first six address ways to get the mental and emotional toxins *out* of your experience. The subsequent nine strategies offer more lighthearted ways to reduce the amount of stress, mental toxins, and emotional clutter coming *in*.

19. TAKE MENTAL INVENTORY

"The person who dumps garbage into your mind will do you considerably more harm than the person who dumps garbage on your floor, because each load of mind garbage negatively impacts your possibilities and lowers your expectations."
– **Zig Ziglar,** author and motivational speaker

What are you feeding your mind? What is your mental and intellectual "nutrition"?

Much like with the "Lay it all out there" strategy, it's helpful to actually see on paper what you feed your mind. So grab a sheet of paper and let's map it out now. For each of the categories below, write down the top 10 you most often consume. For example, under "magazines," list all the magazines you currently subscribe to or read on a regular basis. Do the same for each category:

- Magazines

- Radio programs (news or entertainment)

- Podcasts

- Television shows you regularly watch

- Social media platforms you participate in (Facebook, Twitter, LinkedIn, etc.)

- Blogs you visit

- Email lists you subscribe to

- Newspapers and other forms of news

Once you have your list, go through each item and ask yourself, "Does this magazine/blog/podcast positively and consistently add to my life?" Write "yes" or "no" next to each item.

How do you know if it is positively contributing to your life? Follow up with these questions:

- Is it teaching me something?

- Is it inspiring?

- Is it entertaining?

Then dig a bit deeper. Ask yourself, "For the things I find entertaining, is the content generally positive or negative?"

If the bulk of your news and entertainment is negative, chances are good it is adding to your overall stress level. It is hard to feel calm, peaceful, optimistic, and productive if your mind is bombarded daily with images of drama, doom, and despair.

LIGHTEN YOUR LOAD NOW

- Immediately drop one magazine, podcast, or television show that no longer positively contributes to your life. Drop another one next week, and so on, until the only media left is inspiring, educational, and useful.

20. GO ON A MEDIA-FREE DIET

"There is no lack of time, only a lack of focus and organization."
– **J V Crum,** author of *Conscious Millionaire*

A great way to free up more time and reduce your stress level is to reduce your media consumption. You are likely in front of screens more often than you think. Let's do the numbers.

The average American watches four hours of television per day. This is on top of the time spent surfing the net. So if you watched, on average, four hours of TV per day for the last 30 years, that equals 43,800 hours, which is precisely FIVE YEARS of your life.

Really let that sink in. Five years – poof!

Think of all the things you could have experienced in that time.

Experts in high performance have shown that it takes roughly 10,000 hours to master any subject. Those 43,800 hours spent watching TV could have been used to master four different subjects, like becoming fluent in Russian, a concert pianist, a yoga master, you name it.

When I did this calculation years ago, I was shocked to realize a good six years of my life were spent in front of the tube. So I got rid of the TV altogether, and I have a lot more peace and calm in my life as a result. It may seem counterintuitive, but there is really no such thing as "relaxing" in front of the TV – yet many of us do this as a way to turn off our minds and unwind at the end of the day. The problem is our minds do not turn off. Instead, your mind receives and records everything that is being blasted from the TV. Everything!

While you may not be ready to dump the TV just yet, you can go on a media-free diet.

Try going for a full week without any form of media. That means no TV, internet news, radio, magazines, newspapers, internet surfing, social media, nothing. You might be surprised by how much better you feel and how much more time you have in your day.

LIGHTEN YOUR LOAD NOW

- Experiment with the media-free diet for one week. Notice if you are more productive and less stressed by the end of it.

21. POWER IT DOWN

These days, it's hard to imagine life without texting, smart phones, emails, Facebook, and instant everything. Unfortunately, there are two major downsides to all this electronic connectedness: 1) all this screen time can affect your sleep, and 2) this constant connectedness can cause us to operate in "react or distract" mode. Both translate into more stress.

Let's start with the first one. Not enough quality sleep will put stress on your body and your mind. When you watch TV or work on your computer at night before bed, there's no transition time for your mind to wind down. It will remain active while you're trying to get some shut-eye. Not ideal. You may think you are relaxing in front of the TV, but it's really just more sensory bombardment.

In addition, artificial lights, which include the light coming from your phone, laptop, and tablet, interfere with melatonin production. Melatonin is the sleep hormone that regulates your sleep and wake cycles. The more time spent in front of screens, the more you are potentially interrupting your natural bio-rhythm. Therefore, consider dimming your house lights and powering down your electronics at least an hour before bed to allow your body and mind to register that it's bedtime.

Now to the second one: react and distract mode. While electronic gadgets are convenient, they often hijack our entire day and create an illusion of busyness. In many ways, we've turned into Pavlovian dogs that sit up and take notice of every ring, ding, and ping.

We're addicted. You likely are too.

Don't think so? Consider this. Do you text while you're in the car? What about at the dinner table? How about in the bathroom? There's now a term for that... "shexting." Eew. Are you chatting on the phone while you're standing in front of another human being who's waiting for you to focus and place your latte order?

Still don't think you're addicted? Then try this.

Turn your ringer and all notifications on. That's right. Turn them ALL on. Put the phone somewhere where you can hear it, but where you can't see the screen to know who is calling or texting.

Now, when one of the sound notifications goes off, don't do anything. Don't check to see who it is from. Leave the phone where it is. Notice whether you feel a strong desire to check it.

Just go back to whatever you were doing. Notice how often you get the urge to check your phone to see who or what that text was about. See how long you can go without reaching for the phone AND without *thinking* about reaching for the phone.

The habit of constantly reacting to your phone diverts your focus. Tasks take longer to complete. It's harder to concentrate on your intention and goals for the day when you invite constant interruptions from others.

Recent studies have repeatedly shown that multitasking is *less* efficient, not more. Those "shexters" I mentioned earlier – a good percentage of those phones end up with E-coli bacteria on them.

You cannot give someone your full attention, which is a source of REAL connection, when one of you is messing with the phone.

So what to do?

Consider the "Touch it once" strategy for managing your email inboxes. Schedule a few blocks of time a day where you have time to read and respond to phone calls and texts. Keep the phone off at all other times.

Sounds radical, doesn't it? Or maybe it sounds downright impossible? But what if this one strategy could double your productivity and creativity? What if it could slash your overall stress level? Would it be worth experimenting with it then?

LIGHTEN YOUR LOAD NOW

- For better sleep, power down your electronic gadgets at least an hour before bedtime.

- For increased productivity, as well as more daily peace and calm, schedule time blocks to manage your calls and texts. Keep the phone off at all other times.

22. QUIT COMPLAINING

Have you ever noticed that a lot of our "small talk" and interaction with others centers around complaining?

Somewhere along the way, it has become socially acceptable to voice our constant displeasure about the weather, our daily aches and pains, our relatives, our boss – the list is endless. We seem to almost enjoy commiserating with others by comparing our tales of misery. Somehow the "oh, you think that's bad, how about this" form of one-upmanship has become a form of social bonding. The truth is, all forms of gossiping and negativity are complaints.

Complaining is a toxin.

Complaining is toxic to your mind, to your body, and to those around you. It puts negative energy in your body. You then broadcast that negativity out into the world and draw more negative energy, experiences, and people toward you.

As Will Bowen, author of *A Complaint Free World*, likes to say: "Complaining is like bad breath. We tend to notice when it comes out of someone else's mouth, but not when it comes out of our own." Let's start noticing!

Try to go an entire day without voicing a single complaint. You can think them all you like – if you must – but avoid saying anything negative aloud. Even something as seemingly innocuous as "Boy, it's hot today" is a complaint because you are essentially saying that you wish it weren't so.

LIGHTEN YOUR LOAD NOW

- Try to go an entire day without saying anything negative.

23. DROP THE "SHOULD"

"It's not the load that breaks you down, it's the way you carry it." –
Lou Holtz, former football player and coach

We're constantly adding new words to our daily lexicon. We don't look things up anymore – we "Google" it. We don't just give things – we now "gift" them. If there were a vote on words to *delete* from the dictionary, my vote would go to the word "should."

How often do you think or speak in terms of "should"? How often do "shoulds" creep into your day? You might be surprised by the number of times your mind throws a "should" into your thoughts. High achievers and working moms are especially prone to piling on the "shoulds."

Do any of these ring a bell?

- "I would like to go, but I should finish this first."

- "I should drink more water."

- "I should be more_____ or less _____."

Embedded in the concept of "should" is guilt. When you don't do something you had decided you "should" do, you tend to feel badly about it.

Also mixed in with the idea of "should" is comparison. Comparison invites stress and misery into our lives. In his book *Freedom from the Known*, J. Krishnamurti highlights the dangers of "should" this way: "We are always comparing what we are with what we *should be*. The should-be is a projection of what we think we ought to be. All the time we compare ourselves with those who are richer or more brilliant, more intellectual, more affectionate, more famous, more this and more that. This measuring ourselves all the time against something or someone is one of the primary causes of conflict." And stress.

In addition, "should" is a passive, victim way of looking at the world. It doesn't feel good. Who is it anyway that's telling you that you "should"? Says who? If it's someone else throwing a "should" at you, realize that their "should" has nothing to do with you.

If you've given yourself a "should," recognize that it's not really you who's doing it. Remember the mind we talked about at the start of this chapter? The one that likes to create drama to keep itself occupied? That's typically where the "shoulds" come from – the mind. Luckily, you are not your mind. The *real* you gets to decide whether to listen to that voice or not.

Begin to notice how often you say or think you "should" or "ought to" do anything. Consider dropping the "should" or "ought to" and reframing it with a more empowered way of looking at things. You can replace it with "I choose to do this because…" or "I intend to do this."

LIGHTEN YOUR LOAD NOW

> - Notice how often you speak or think in terms of "should" or "ought to." Mentally reframe it by saying "I choose to" or "I want to because…" instead.

24. STOP WORRYING

"We can easily manage if we will only take, each day, the burden appointed to it. But the load will be too heavy for us if we carry yesterday's burden over again today, and then add the burden of the morrow before we are required to bear it."
– **John Newton,** former Anglican preacher

Worrying helps no one. In fact, it makes everything worse. Think about that for a moment.

Worrying can make you physically sick. It pollutes your mind and body and spreads to everything and everyone around you. It's like pouring negativity on an already stressful situation. It activates the production of cortisol – the stress hormone – in your body.

Plus, the object of your worrying is not helped by it one bit. Worry is not productive or helpful. It's equivalent to praying for what you don't want.

Studies have shown that less than 10 percent of worries are justified. The rest either never materialize or they are about things we cannot do anything about, such as the past or other people's business.

Some part of us must think worrying serves a useful purpose, or else why would we do it? It's the mind that thinks this – and the mind loves addiction. Worrying is an addiction.

How to stop worrying? The key to breaking this addiction is to realize when it is happening and to replace it with something else.

Start monitoring your thoughts more closely. It's all about awareness. See if you can catch yourself when you take off on the negative, worry-wart train. Forget about what *might* happen. What's happening in THIS moment? Forget about what you *don't* want. What is it that you DO want?

When you find yourself in the midst of a worry thought, stop and take a couple of deep breaths. Is there an action you could take to remedy this situation? If yes, then take that action immediately. If not, continue to breathe deeply as you visualize what you DO want. Visualize it until you can feel it as if it were happening now. The key is to really *feel* it.

LIGHTEN YOUR LOAD NOW

- Begin to notice when you enter a state of worry. Take several deep breaths and turn it around by visualizing the specifics of what you DO want.

25. RELAX YOUR FACE

"Sometimes the simple things are the most profound."
– Karin Kiser

When in the midst of a stressful thought or moment, or when your mind is racing from one thing to the next, stop and focus on your face.

We carry an enormous amount of tension in our face. Your jaw might be clenched and your brow might be furrowed as you read this. See if you can notice any facial tension right now. It may not feel like anything is tense, but that doesn't mean it isn't. Sometimes we only become aware of how much tension we are holding after we consciously relax it. Let's practice this now.

Sit up straight with your feet on the floor. Take a couple of deep breaths to prepare. Now, you will take seven deep breaths, and with each breath, you will relax a part of your face. For example:

- Breath # 1: As you inhale, visualize relaxing energy flooding into your body. As you exhale, direct that relaxing energy to your forehead. Relax your forehead as much as possible.

- Breath # 2: Do the same with the inhale. Visualize more relaxing energy flooding into your body. On the exhale, direct that energy to your eyebrows. Soften your eyebrows as you relax them.

- Breath # 3: Follow the pattern above, this time focusing on your eyes.

- Breath # 4: Cheeks

- Breath # 5: Jaw

- Breath # 6: Mouth

- Breath # 7: Lips

After you have relaxed each part of your face, try smiling. Smiling, even forced smiling, can decrease your stress level and give a welcome boost to your health and happiness.

Don't feel like smiling? Then stick out your tongue instead. Way out. Doing so will stretch your jaw and face muscles. Plus, you might feel so silly doing it that you end up genuinely smiling in spite of yourself.

LIGHTEN YOUR LOAD NOW

- When you find yourself in the middle of a stressful thought or situation, pause and take several deep breaths. Relax a different part of your face with each exhale.

- Smile for no reason. Even a forced smile has health benefits.

26. ADOPT AN ATTITUDE OF GRATITUDE

Our attitude is an amazing tool – when we consciously use it. We choose our attitude. When we adopt a positive attitude and expect things to turn out well, they typically do. When we adopt an attitude of gratitude for the people, things, and experiences already in our lives, we tend to attract more people, things, and experiences to be grateful for. It's the basic Law of Attraction at work.

How many times a day do you say "thank you," either silently or aloud? Can you quickly name five things you are grateful for? How about 10 things?

More gratitude = less stress.

It's easier to adopt an attitude of gratitude if you add it to your morning routine. Start the day with gratitude, even before your feet touch the floor!

Rather than waking up each morning and immediately jumping into your routine, your to-do list, or your electronic gadgets, consider taking 60 seconds – while you are still in bed – to name a few things you are grateful for. You might be amazed at how this one simple practice can shift the tone of your entire day.

As you move about your day, consider how everything adds to your experience. You can even say a silent "thank you" to yourself when you notice things. You happen to catch the sunrise…"thank you." You have a reliable car that gets you from A to B…"thank you." Someone at work pays you a compliment…"thank you." And as you lie in your warm, soft bed at night…"thank you."

LIGHTEN YOUR LOAD NOW

> - Monitor how many times you say "thank you" today. Consider how you might double that number.

27. MEDITATE

Meditation is an excellent way to relax, quiet the mind, and reduce your stress level. Even taking one minute several times a day to sit quietly and follow the breath can do wonders. You don't have to limit yourself to silent meditations, though. Some find it helpful to listen to a guided meditation or have soft music playing in the background to keep the mind focused so it doesn't stray off on endless tangents.

No time to sit and meditate, you say? Can't seem to turn off the looping thoughts? Or perhaps you have convinced yourself that you're not good at meditating? That was definitely my excuse a few years ago. I was good at reading *about* meditation and not so good at actually setting aside the time to practice it. My mind would try to convince me that it was a waste of time or wouldn't work for me.

Another common mind tactic is to tell yourself you will meditate once all the other stuff on your to-do list is done, which essentially guarantees you'll never do it. Why? Because the other stuff is NEVER done. The whole point of meditation is to go *beyond* the mind. The mind knows this, so it will inevitably set up roadblocks at first. Don't get discouraged.

There is no right or wrong way to meditate. The idea is simply to turn off all distractions and just be with yourself, noticing whatever happens to come up. If your mind keeps jumping from thought to thought, just notice that.

Almost anything can be a meditation if you bring your full awareness to it. Experiment with different methods and music to find what really resonates with you. For years, I did all my meditating and deep contemplating while walking. Even before I knew what meditating was, I would go for a walk whenever I needed to clear my head. I just instinctively knew to do this. No matter what problem I had or how foul my mood, by the end of the walk, I felt better and often had the solution to the problem. What is your preferred way to clear your head and access deeper wisdom?

What's common to all types of meditation is that they center and ground you. Meditation interrupts the addiction to being super busy with jam-packed days. It opens more space in your mind so you have room for new ideas and creative inspiration.

Not sure where to start? Try this five-minute meditation.

Set a kitchen timer or alarm for five minutes. Sit in a comfy chair with your feet firmly planted on the floor, hands in your lap. Keep your back straight and shoulders relaxed. Close your eyes and just BE. If a thought comes to you, just observe it like a cloud passing by. Whenever you find yourself returning to thinking mode, just gently bring your attention back to your breathing. Take slow inhalations and exhalations. Some people find it helpful to count the length of each breath as a way to distract the mind from other thoughts. On each inhale, visualize the healing and grounding energy coming up from the core of the Earth through the bottom of your feet and up throughout your body. On the exhale, visualize all stress, negativity, and fatigue rushing down your body and out your feet, down to the Earth's core, where it is instantly neutralized.

LIGHTEN YOUR LOAD NOW

- Experiment with a five-minute meditation every day for a week. Need help? Download a free guided meditation audio from below link.

  http://karinkiser.com/free-gifts/

Breathing Reminder

OK, at the risk of sounding like a broken record, this is yet another reminder to stop and breathe – at least a few times during the day.

Why do I keep mentioning this? Two reasons: 1) Because it works. You can cleanse your mind and detox your body by spending just ONE minute, several times a day, with your breath, and 2) Because as much as I personally know about the benefits of deep and conscious breathing, I still find myself forgetting to do it – often for days at a time!

On an intellectual level, I know that conscious breathing is one of the keys to freeing your life of stress and toxins, and yet I often forget to do it consistently. That's why it is important to link it with an activity you already do, such as taking a shower or waiting at a stop light. You could also take a few conscious breaths before every meeting, at the top of every hour, before eating a meal, or before sending an email. Pick one activity to remind yourself to stop and breathe.

Now, before reading any further, let's stop right now and take a few deep breaths.

Ahhh.

28. MIX IT UP

When the mind has nothing better to do, it will create drama in your life. You can minimize this tendency of the mind by mixing things up! That means breaking up some of your habits and daily routines. You may not even realize that much of your day is on autopilot.

For example, do you start your day the same way, at the same time, day in and day out? Have you ever noticed that you do things like brushing your teeth or putting on a shirt the same way every time? The same arm goes in first, the same shoelace gets tied first. We do this unconsciously. It requires no conscious thought.

Or what about this? Have you ever pulled into your driveway, only to realize you have no memory of the drive home? Because it requires no conscious thought, your mind is free to wander and make mischief.

With the "Mix it up" strategy, you pick one routine activity and do it differently. For example, take another route to work, just because. When grocery shopping, avoid parking in the usual area and making your way through the store the same way you always do. Mix it up by parking far away, taking a different route through the store, and buying something new!

Try writing a note with the opposite hand. Better yet, try brushing your teeth with your other hand. You'll quickly discover just how much concentration is needed!

When you mix things up, you become more alive. You use more of your senses. Look at young children or remember back to when you were four or five years old. Sure, there might have been some basic structure and routine, like when to eat meals and when to take a nap, but on the whole, every moment was new and exciting. There were so many new things to explore and learn.

When you regularly mix things up and alter your routine, you can tap into this childlike sense of wonder that is still inside you – even if it's currently buried under a boatload of stress, routine, and obligations.

Consider how you can be more present and alive in what you normally do. Consider how you might incorporate some newness into your day. Need some ideas?

- Strike up a conversation with a total stranger while in line at the grocery store, post office, or coffee shop.

- Pick a new restaurant to try, preferably one that serves a type of food you have never eaten before.

- Park in a different spot at work.

- Say hello to everyone you pass in the office.

- Use your non-dominant hand for everything today: brushing your teeth, opening doors, eating, etc.

- Sign up for that dance class you have thought about for years.

- Visit a park you've never been to.

The possibilities are endless!

LIGHTEN YOUR LOAD NOW

- Challenge yourself to see how many routine things you can do differently today. Include any new things as well. At the end of the day, notice how much different you feel.

29. GO OUTSIDE!

In Chapter Three, we learned that the average American spends 87 percent of her life indoors. Well, another six percent is spent in automobiles, which leaves only a measly seven percent spent outdoors! That's just a few hours per week!

Cleaner air isn't the only reason to go outside on a regular basis. Going outside can boost your mood, calm your anxiety, and reduce your stress level. In fact, studies have shown that even looking outside or at nature photos can have a positive effect on your mood.

Need a few more reasons to go outside?

- Pain relief: The earth is like one giant anti-inflammatory. If you have a headache, a backache, indigestion, or are just feeling fatigued, go outside and place your bare feet directly on the grass, dirt, sand, or concrete. Notice how you feel after about 20 minutes.

- Vitamin D boost: Vitamin D3 is crucial for bone health and plays an important role in protecting against a number of chronic diseases. Your body produces it naturally when your skin is exposed to sunlight (without the sunscreen).

- Relaxation and mental clarity: When you step into nature, you enter a world that's bigger than you and certainly bigger than your problems. Being outdoors in nature can quickly put things in their proper perspective. As you become one with your surroundings, you sense and feel more. Your eyes get a welcome break from the focused, up-close work in front of computers and inside cubicles. You can feel the sun and the breeze on your face. You relax into your true nature. Nature is part of *your* nature.

Spending time outside every day is especially important if you work in a windowless office building all day. Try eating your lunch outside or taking a walk during your lunch break. Get outside as much as you can, even if it means sitting outside your house for five minutes before heading off to work.

LIGHTEN YOUR LOAD NOW

- Schedule a daily nature fix, even if it's just for 15 minutes.

30. TOUCH SOMETHING

Who or what have you lovingly touched today? Perhaps you kissed your spouse, hugged your child, or pet your dog. Maybe you touched the plants in your garden.

Physical touch plays a role in reducing not only your mental and emotional toxins, but also the effects of any new stressors heading your way.

Physical touch is all about creating a connection. That connection doesn't have to be just with people. We already explored in the last strategy how touching the earth with your bare feet can offer health benefits. You can connect with the energy and spirit of the earth as well. You can also connect with plants – and trees – and just about everything.

So today, touch something. Touch a tree. Pet someone else's dog. Kiss your kids. Hug someone for just a second or two longer than you normally would.

LIGHTEN YOUR LOAD NOW

- Touch something today with love and kindness.

31. DO SOMETHING FUN

How often do you jump up and down, skip all around, or throw your arms up in the air like you just don't care?

Ever wonder why kids like to spin around and around until they practically fall over? Because it's fun! What have *you* done this week that was purely for fun? Sorry, watching television doesn't count. Neither does eating.

It qualifies as fun if it lights you up – if it's amusing, lighthearted, creative, or playful. It qualifies as fun if there's a sense of adventure or newness to it.

Imagine if someone were to come up to you and say, "Quick! Name five things you love to do for fun." Could you do it? Or would you draw a blank?

Having fun – and having fun often – is important. Just like the new practices of deep breathing, mini meditations, and going outside, incorporating some play time into your week allows your body and mind to relax, reset, and rejuvenate. You'll reap the benefits even if it's only for a few minutes a day. After all, what's the point of our brief ride on planet Earth if we aren't enjoying the journey?

Right about now, you might be thinking, "I can't have fun, or even think about having fun, when I'm stressed out by my (job, coworkers, to-do list, spouse, kids, in-laws, finances, insert-your-reason-here)." Maybe you believe there is no time for fun. Or that somehow you don't deserve it. Or that there will be plenty of time for that later. Those beliefs are mental toxins. They add to your stress load.

Years ago, back in my 70+ hour work weeks, a new acquaintance asked me what I liked to do for fun. I didn't have an answer. I had forgotten all about fun. That was a wake-up call. It had been so long since I'd had any free time that I couldn't think of what I would do if I had some. So I decided to take a thorough inventory.

I made a list of the fun things I had ever done or experienced. I thought back to the fun I had as a kid. I even pulled out old photos, scrapbooks, and diaries to jog my memory. Then I considered whether I would still enjoy any of those things now. And then I took action. I called up a friend and scheduled a play date to revisit miniature golf and Skee-Ball. I picked up dancing again. I bought some grown-up coloring books and some fancy pens. Let the play time begin!

Now it's your turn. Think back to your childhood. What did you absolutely love to do? Did you like to color, jump rope, skateboard, play kickball, dance, play board games, ride your bike, go exploring, tell stories, play with your pets, build stuff, or make up games with the other kids?

Make a list of at least five things you enjoyed as a kid. Think about *why* you liked each of those things. Was it the imagination and creativity? The adventure and exploration? The sense of belonging in a group? How could you incorporate some of those things now?

Start by picking one thing and enlisting a fun buddy to do it with you.

LIGHTEN YOUR LOAD NOW

- Call up a friend and schedule a play date this week, even if it's only for an hour.

32. DECIDE TO BE HAPPY

Happiness is a decision.

Notice your immediate reaction to reading that. Was it similar to one of these?

- "Yeah, right."

- "I *would* be happy, if only _____ happened."

- "Sure, easy for you to say. You don't have to deal with _____."

If you've been skipping around in the book, and this is one of the first ways to **Lighten Your Load** you have read, then I can understand your skepticism. Bear with me a moment.

Just like you can decide what to eat for breakfast, how to organize your desk, and what news and information you feed your mind with, you can choose to make happiness a day-by-day and moment-by-moment decision as well.

Happiness is a choice. It's a mindset and an attitude – and you can change yours at any moment. That's great news! You are responsible! The choice is yours.

You can choose now to appreciate what you already have. You can choose your friends and the people you surround yourself with. You can choose to think in terms of "want to" instead of "ought to."

You can choose happiness too.

Take a moment to visualize yourself as happy, right now. What would that look like? Who else would be there? More importantly, how would you feel? Really picture it and feel how that would feel in your body.

Your mind doesn't know the difference between what is real and what is imagined, so as spiritual teacher Osho says, "Imagine yourself as happy as possible. Within a week you will start feeling that you are becoming very happy for no reason at all."[2] The more you do this, the more you train the mind to believe it. The mind will then look for evidence to support that belief.

LIGHTEN YOUR LOAD NOW

- Imagine yourself as ridiculously happy. Do it as often as possible, especially first thing in the morning and just before bed.

33. CELEBRATE THE SUCCESSES

We don't celebrate our successes nearly as much as we could. Have you ever noticed this?

We can go crazy with excitement when toddlers do small things like put toys away or eat all their peas, yet we diminish our own accomplishments. We do it all the time.

We cross another thing off our to-do list and immediately go on to the next thing without acknowledging our progress or really feeling good about the thing we just crossed off the list.

Let's pause for a moment and find something to celebrate. Grab a piece of paper and write down 10 major successes you have experienced in your life thus far. Don't worry if this exercise takes a few minutes. Sadly, it's easy to forget about even our major milestones. Did you pay your way through college, for example? Yay for you! That's a big one. Write it down.

Have you helped someone in need, earned an award or a promotion, or overcome a tragedy, loss, fear, or illness? Those count too.

Did you try a new hobby or sport that you've been wanting to for years? Did you keep your heart open and vulnerable to love even though it had been broken before? Did you decide to forgive someone so *you* could heal? Write it all down and place the list where you can see it.

Now let's look at your everyday successes. Name five successes you have already experienced today. It doesn't matter how small they may seem. Did you have a great night's sleep? Feel good about that. Did you take a couple of deep, conscious breaths before starting your car to drive to the office? Have you already completed the number one item on your agenda for today? Then celebrate that!

Now, when I say "celebrate," I don't mean go out and buy a pint of ice cream and eat it all in one sitting. That's essentially justifying a self-sabotaging habit that will ultimately make you feel worse. True celebration involves acknowledging, appreciating, loving, and nurturing yourself, not from a place of ego, but from a place of gratitude.

Me, I like to jump up and down. I've also been known to clap my hands together for a few seconds and say "yay" while driving. Or I'll throw my arms over my head wildly as I walk upstairs. Sure, it's silly – but it makes me feel good, and that's the whole point – to feel good about YOU.

Stop and celebrate the fact that you've read this far in the book. Have you taken any of the *Lighten Your Load* action steps from the 32 ways we have covered so far? Even if you've taken only a tiny step toward just one of them, that's progress. Celebrate that!

There is always something to celebrate if you look for it.

LIGHTEN YOUR LOAD NOW

> - Write out your successes at the end of each day – no matter how small they may seem. Aim for a minimum of 10. Then promptly celebrate!

7 | LIGHTEN YOUR LOAD ON THE PLANET

It might seem strange to have a chapter on the planet in a book about lightening YOUR load. After all, it's YOU who is stressed out.

The reality is – we are not separate from our environment.

It's not just *your* stress, toxins, and clutter. We're sharing this "life garbage" with the planet as well, and it's coming right back to us in the form of more polluted air, water, and food.

The plastics we use end up in the ocean. The fish eat the plastic, and then we eat those fish. Many of the cleaners and chemicals we wash down the drain – and the pharmaceuticals we pee out – come right back to us in the water supply. Our negative, fearful, and destructive thoughts are broadcast to the world, and they come right back to us in many forms.

Much like in our own lives, we can become overwhelmed by the magnitude of what's happening to the planet we live on. Temperatures are rising, the ice caps are melting, and there are holes in the ozone layer. Human beings are bulldozing forests, destroying rainforests, and driving countless species to extinction like never before. What can one person do to make a difference when we're still trying to keep it together in our own lives?

Just as there is no single, all-encompassing way to free your life of stress, toxins, and clutter, there's no single strategy to detox and declutter the planet either. There is a lot we can do, however. This chapter alone could include 35 ways, but for now, we'll start with two. One is simple and easy to implement, and the other will likely stretch you beyond your comfort zone.

34. BRING YOUR OWN

In Chapter Four, Lighten Your Load of Stuff, you may have noticed I suggested either donating or recycling your excess stuff. I purposely did not recommend just throwing it away. Why? Unfortunately, there is no such thing as AWAY. "Away" does not exist.

Each person generates an average of 4.4 pounds (2 kilograms) of garbage per day,[1] which pollutes the land, air, and water. Recycling is not enough. The core of the problem is that we consume too much and generate too much waste.

Everything we throw away either ends up incinerated or in a landfill. Both burning it and burying it add to the toxic load of the planet. The processes of burning and burying reintroduce contaminants into the soil, into the air we breathe, and into the water – all of which end up in the food and beverages we consume.

So lightening our load on the planet means minimizing the amount of trash we generate. Plain and simple. One of the largest contributors to this mounting pile of waste is the daily disposables – the things we use on a daily basis that get tossed out after a single use, or if we're lucky, a second use. That includes all plastic water bottles, to-go coffee cups, all takeout containers, and shopping bags of all kinds. Sure, you may recycle a lot of this, but the reality is that 1) not all of it is recyclable in the first place, and 2) not everything you place in the recycle bin is actually recycled.

So the obvious solution is to bring your own, starting with your own bag, coffee mug, and water bottle. Let's explore each of these in turn.

Bag

According to the City of San Diego's Environmental Services Department, 500 million plastic bags are distributed every year in the city. Each of these is used on average for 12 minutes.[2] And that's just in one city! In the European Union, more than 3.4 million tons of plastic carrier bags are produced each year, which amounts to the weight of more than two million cars.[3]

Bringing your own reusable bag translates to 50 percent less energy, a 40 percent reduction in greenhouse gas emissions, and 30 percent less water than a single-use plastic bag – and that's after only eight uses of the reusable bag.[4] Perhaps you already bring your own bag to the supermarket or farmers' market. Wonderful! Do you also bring it with you to the office supply store? To the pet store? What about – dare I say – the shopping mall?

Coffee Mug

How many disposable beverage cups do you use and discard each week? It's probably more than you think. Be sure to count the coffee cups, lunch takeout cups, and the water dispenser cups at the office. You might be surprised to know that Starbucks beverages alone account for four billion cups globally each year.[5] That's billion with a B. And that's just one beverage company. Most paper to-go coffee cups cannot be recycled due to the plastic coating on the inside. The lid might be recyclable, but the cup itself typically is not. How often do you see anyone separate the top from the cup and throw each away separately?

Even if you could recycle the whole thing, the reality is that not everyone recycles. The bigger issue is that we have become a "throw away" culture. Recycling is still throwing it out; it's just throwing it out in a greener way. Reusing would be the more sustainable way.

Consider bringing your own mug for that midday latte or morning cup of joe. You'll avoid all possible chemical leaching from those heated plastic lids, and your coffee will likely taste better. Some coffee shops even offer a cup discount when you bring your own mug.

Water Bottle

The other biggie is plastic water bottles. They are everywhere. I get it. In many places, you wouldn't want to drink water from the local tap. That's all the more reason to bring your own – in a glass or metal container – wherever you go.

As we saw in Chapter Three, more than 60 million water bottles are thrown away each day in the United States alone. Only about 17 percent are recycled.[6] The rest are buried in landfills, where they can take up to 1,000 years to biodegrade, burned in incinerators, where they release toxic by-products into the air, or simply left as litter.

LIGHTEN YOUR LOAD NOW

- Take a reusable water bottle wherever you go, which also helps with strategy # 1 "Drink enough water."

- Consider keeping a reusable bag and coffee mug in your car and at the office.

35. EAT MORE PLANTS

What does eating more plants and fewer animal products have to do with helping the planet? Surprisingly, a lot. It takes an enormous amount of the planet's resources to grow, graze, and feed the animals that end up on our dinner plates.

For example, it takes a whopping 2,000 gallons of water to produce just one pound of beef. It also takes roughly 1,000 gallons of water to produce a single gallon of milk. That's a lot of water! Just growing the crops that we feed to livestock consumes *half of the entire water use in the United States.*[7] That means that the water we're saving by taking quicker showers and watering our front lawns less frequently is really just a drop in the bucket compared to the amount of water we use to produce the animal products we eat and drink every day.

It's not just the water supply that suffers. The air we breathe takes a toll as well. It has been shown that animal agriculture contributes as much pollution in the form of methane and carbon dioxide as *all forms of transportation combined.*[8]

So what can you do about this? You could switch to a plant-based diet – right now. (I warned you this one might be beyond your comfort zone.) You can live more lightly on the planet, right now, by upgrading the way you eat. Your mind will likely object to this. I bet it can easily rattle off 10 reasons why changing your diet is either a bad idea or downright impossible. That's what the mind does. Luckily, you are not your mind. The *real* you can do anything.

As a first step, take inventory of what you currently eat in a typical week. Write it all down. Consider these questions:

- How much of what you eat is genuine nutrition for your body's cells?

- How much of it is just "filler"?

- Refer back to strategy # 11 "Eat your L's." How much of your food is local, live, and light?

- How much of it energizes you?

- How much of what you eat makes you feel tired, bloated, or heavy?

- How many animal products do you consume each day? Animal products such as meat and dairy are highly acidic to the body, which means they can lead to inflammation and stress.

Consider replacing some of that filler and some of those animal products with nutrient-dense, plant-based superfoods, things like coconut, blueberries, spirulina, cacao, goji berries, and hemp seeds. Experiment with new foods like quinoa, kale, and seaweeds. Mix it up! Not only will you lighten your load on the planet, but you just might lighten yourself of a few unwanted pounds as well!

LIGHTEN YOUR LOAD NOW

- Replace today's filler foods with nutrient-dense, plant-based alternatives.

- Experiment with one totally new food this week.

8 | BRINGING IT ALL TOGETHER

As you can see, there's a lot more to toxins and clutter than a crowded closet or a constipated colon. What we put in, on, and around our bodies and minds also adds to the load. Cellular toxins, physical clutter, and mental and emotional stress – they all interfere with your natural state of inner calm, joy, and ease.

As I mentioned in Chapter One, stress is a symptom. There are plenty of sources of stress that we didn't directly address here, such as family stress, work stress, and financial stress. It isn't the events themselves or the individual people that CAUSE us stress. Stress comes from our internal – and often automatic – reaction to them. You can change how you react to stressful thoughts, people, and events. You do this by changing what you put in your body, your mind, and your personal space.

Toxic body = toxic thoughts

When you reduce the amount of physical toxins that creep into your body over time, you feel better. You sleep better. You think more clearly. You have more patience. You handle stress more calmly.

Uncluttered space = uncluttered mind

When you simplify your personal environment of excess and un-needed stuff, you literally create space for more of what you really want in life.

Change your thoughts = change your reality

When you upgrade your "mental nutrition" and bring greater awareness to the way you think and speak, you create a protective barrier around you that wards off negativity, complainers, and your own fear-based thoughts. This frees up more time and energy for the things that are truly important to you.

Now let's bring it all together and review the strategies we've covered for clearing and upgrading your body, mind, and personal space.

DETOX – LIGHTEN YOUR CELLULAR AND PHYSICAL LOAD

1. **Drink Enough Water:** Divide your body weight in half. Aim to drink that amount in ounces each day. Monitor the color of your urine to know when more water is needed.

2. **Add Lemon for Your Liver:** Add freshly-squeezed organic lemon juice to your glass of room-temperature water.

3. **Cleanse:** Add more fiber to your diet. Consider a group cleanse program for more hands-on support.

4. **Brush Your Skin:** Get a dry skin brush made from natural fibers and use it daily for 15 minutes.

5. **Sweat:** Pick one new sweaty action to incorporate this week, preferably while wearing organic clothing (unless, of course, your sweaty action is a bath or sauna!).

6. **Breathe Deeply:** Add a few conscious breaths to your daily routine by linking it with an activity you already do. Pause and take a few deep breaths first thing in the morning, before you start your car, while waiting at a stop light, before or after every meeting – you get the idea.

7. **Open the Windows:** Let the fresh air in, especially when cooking, cleaning, or using paint or other chemical-based hobby supplies.

8. **Move Your Body:** Incorporate one five-minute movement break into each day this week. Increase it to two next week.

9. **Upgrade Your Water:** Drink the best water you can find, preferably out of a glass, metal, or ceramic container.

10. **Get a Shower Filter:** Enough said.

11. **Eat Your L's:** Eat local, live, and light. You'll live longer, and leaner, while living lightly on the planet.

12. **Go Natural:** The next time you run out of a personal care item like toothpaste, body lotion, or shampoo, upgrade to a more natural alternative.

DECLUTTER – LIGHTEN YOUR LOAD OF STUFF

13. **Clear Your Clutter:** Identify the top 10 areas in your home or office that could use some decluttering and then tackle the smallest one this week. Then promptly celebrate your success.

14. **Wear it or Donate it:** If it doesn't currently fit you, if you haven't worn it in years, or if you aren't willing to wear it now, it's a prime candidate for the donation pile.

15. **Never Buy Another Hanger:** Keep three empty hangers and donate the rest. When all hangers are occupied, purchase a new clothing item only when you are prepared to donate another item you already have.

16. **Lay it All Out There:** Empty out all the kitchen cupboards or your hall closet. Spread the contents around the room so you can take a good look at all you have. Return each item to its hiding place only AFTER you have used it.

17. **Spring Clean Your Inbox:** Start small. Schedule one 30-minute chunk of time when you can tackle your inbox with the delete button. Look for quick and obvious things you can delete or unsubscribe from, such as ads, forwarded chain mail, and old invitations.

18. **Touch it Once:** Check your email and snail mail only when you are prepared to act on it, right then.

DE-STRESS – LIGHTEN YOUR MENTAL AND EMOTIONAL LOAD

19. **Take Mental Inventory:** Drop one magazine, podcast, or television show that no longer positively contributes to your life.

20. **Go on a Media-Free Diet:** Go media-free for one solid week. Notice if you are more productive and less stressed by the end of it.

21. **Power it Down:** Schedule time blocks to manage your calls and texts. For optimal sleep, power down your electronic gadgets at least an hour before bedtime.

22. **Quit Complaining:** Try to go an entire day without saying anything negative.

23. **Drop the "Should":** Notice today how often you speak or think in terms of "should" or "ought to." Mentally reframe it with "I choose to" or "I want to because…" instead.

24. **Stop Worrying:** Try to catch yourself when you start to worry. Take several deep breaths and turn it around by visualizing the specifics of what you DO want.

25. **Relax Your Face:** Smile for no reason. Even a forced smile has health benefits.

26. **Adopt an Attitude of Gratitude:** Monitor how many times you say "thank you" today. Consider how you might double that number.

27. **Meditate:** Experiment with a five-minute meditation every day for a week. Download a free guided meditation from http://karinkiser.com/free-gifts/

28. **Mix it Up:** Challenge yourself to see how many routine things you can do differently today. At the end of the day, notice how much different you feel.

29. **Go Outside!** Schedule a daily nature fix, even if it's just 15 minutes during your lunch break.

30. **Touch Something:** Hug, kiss, pet, or touch something or someone today with love and kindness.

31. **Do Something Fun:** Call up a friend and schedule a play date this week, even if it's only for an hour.

32. **Decide to Be Happy:** Imagine yourself as ridiculously happy. Do it as often as possible, especially first thing in the morning and just before bed.

33. **Celebrate the Successes:** Write out your successes at the end of each day – no matter how small they may seem. Aim for a minimum of 10. Then promptly celebrate!

LIGHTEN YOUR LOAD ON THE PLANET

34. **Bring Your Own:** Take a reusable water bottle wherever you go. Keep a reusable bag and coffee mug in your car and at the office.

35. **Eat More Plants:** Replace today's filler food with plant-based, nutrient-dense alternatives. Experiment with one totally new food this week.

So there you have it – 35 sometimes simple, sometimes radical ways to *Lighten Your Load.* Not all of the strategies will appeal to you. That's perfectly okay. It's not about how many strategies you try, it's about which ones you practice consistently over time. Pick the ones that resonate most with you.

You might have noticed that many of the above action steps involve noticing. Noticing, monitoring, paying attention – these are all forms of awareness. Dare to be aware! Bringing greater awareness to what you put in, on, and around your body makes it that much harder for the toxins, clutter, and other life garbage to creep back in. Start to notice why you *really* buy something. Become aware of how much of what you think, say, and do comes from a place of "should," complaints, or worry.

Life is largely a matter of paying attention AND taking inspired action.

Start with one technique that appeals to you, and practice it until it becomes a natural part of your day. Then add another. Consistency is key. If you would like a free tool to help you remember the 35 strategies and track your daily and weekly progress, download the *Lighten Your Load* Success Tracker from
http://karinkiser.com/free-gifts/

To keep you motivated, consider getting a friend or coworker to be your accountability buddy. Give them a copy of the book, and check in with them weekly to go over your progress and celebrate your successes, no matter how small.

Let's celebrate right now. By reading this book, you have taken a huge step toward a more peaceful, healthy, and spacious life. How do you feel?

It's time to start noticing!

Notes

Chapter Three

1. Andrew M. Pope, Meta A. Snyder, and Lillian H. Mood, Editors. *Nursing, Health, and the Environment.* (Washington, D.C.: National Academy Press, 1995).

2. Barbara Wren. *Cellular Awakening.* (Carlsbad, CA: Hay House, Inc., 2009).

3. Joseph Mercola. "Dry Skin Brushing: Benefits and How To." *Mercola.com.* February 24, 2014. http://articles.mercola.com/sites/articles/archive/2014/02/24/dry-skin-brushing.aspx

4. Michael Wood. "Is 10 Minutes of Jumping Rope Equivalent to Running 30 Minutes?" *Michael Wood Fitness.* September 21, 2013. http://michaelwoodblog.com/2013/09/21/850/

Chapter Four

1. "National Drinking Water Database." *Environmental Working Group.* December 2009. http://www.ewg.org/tap-water/executive-summary.php

2. Yang CZ, Yaniger SI, Jordan VC, Klein DJ, Bittner GD. "Most Plastic Products Release Estrogenic Chemicals: A Potential Health Problem That Can Be Solved." *Environmental Health Perspectives.* 2011.

3. "Food and Agriculture – Bottled Water Consumption in the United States, 1976-2007." *Earth Policy Institute.* http://www.earth-policy.org/data_center/C24

4. Fox, Catherine Clarke. "Drinking Water: Bottled or From the Tap." *National Geographic,* 2011. http://kids.nationalgeographic.com/kids/stories/spacescience/water-bottle-pollution/

5. "Plastics Facts and Stats." *Container Recycling Institute.* http://www.container-recycling.org/index.php/factsstatistics/plastic

Chapter Six

1. Osho. *Emotional Wellness.* (New York: Harmony Books, 2007).

2. Osho. *Pharmacy for the Soul.* (New York: St. Martin's Griffin, 2004).

Chapter Seven

1. "Municipal Solid Waste." *U.S. Environmental Protection Agency.* http://www3.epa.gov/epawaste/nonhaz/municipal/

2. Environmental Services Department. "Bring Your Own Bag San Diego." *The City of San Diego.* http://www.sandiego.gov/environmental-services/recycling/byobsd/

3. "Bag Free World." http://www.plasticbagfreeday.org/content/facts/

4. Environmental Services Department. "Bring Your Own Bag San Diego." *The City of San Diego.* http://www.sandiego.gov/environmental-services/recycling/byobsd/

5. "Goals & Progress: Cup Recycling." *Starbucks.* http://www.starbucks.com/responsibility/global-report/environmental-stewardship/cup-recycling

6. "Plastics Facts and Stats." *Container Recycling Institute.* http://www.container-recycling.org/index.php/factsstatistics/plastic

7. "The Facts." *Cowspiracy: The Sustainability Secret.* http://www.cowspiracy.com/facts/

8. Ibid.

Acknowledgements

I was inspired to create a group cleanse program when several long-term clients in my Pilates practice witnessed my own "toxicity to vitality" process and wanted a similar experience. That was level 1. Five of those clients – Diann, Elizabeth, Michele, Pamela, and Patty – continued the journey with me with the deeper level programs that followed – level 2, then level 3, then 3.5, then 4. I was learning right along with them and am deeply grateful for their trust in me and in the process. This book is a result of our work together. Thank you!

Most of the writing for this book was done on a bench in the San Diego Botanic Garden, an idyllic 37-acre home away from home that serves as my creative and nurturing sanctuary. Thank you, nature!

I am grateful for the many mentors and heart-centered entrepreneurs who have helped me clarify my purpose and step into a greater role in the world: Baeth Davis, Sabine Messner, Pamelah Landers, Steve Jack, Ryan Eliason, and Rich German among many others.

To the spiritual teachers and authors who have most inspired and guided me along the path: David Hawkins, Osho, Paolo Coelho, Wayne Dyer, Eckhart Tolle, Sonia Choquette, Panache Desai and Michael Singer.

To my book launch team: for their fabulous feedback, brainstorming sessions, and efforts to rally the promotional troops.

Thanks to Mom and Dad, who had essentially the same response when I announced I was writing a book: "You go, girl" from Mom, and "Go, Karin, go" from Dad.

And thanks also to the fundants. You know who you are.

About The Author

KARIN KISER is the founder of Radical Simplicity™ and creator of the Ultimate Life and Body Reboot program. She helps professional and health-conscious women simplify and detox their lives so they can live at a higher level with more time, energy, simplicity, and ease. As a visionary and mentor, she inspires women to greater health and happiness by teaching them to reduce the physical, mental, and emotional toxins blocking their path. She has worked with hundreds of women individually to reduce stress, lighten their load, laugh more, breathe more, and BE more.

A former corporate executive and Pilates studio owner, Karin is on a mission to help people live lives of joy, radiant health and sustainability, for themselves and for the planet. Find out more about her work at www.KarinKiser.com.

Wait!

Before You Go, Don't Forget To Get Your FREE Gifts...

- The Top 5 Tips To Implement Now
- The Lighten Your Load Success Tracker
- Your Special 5 Minute Guided Meditation

Each of These 3 Free Gifts Will Help You On Your Journey To Lighten Your Load.

To Get Them Visit:
http://karinkiser.com/free-gifts/

Made in the USA
San Bernardino, CA
15 February 2016